Waterfowling
These
Past Fifty Years

David Hagerbaumer

Forewords by
M. D. Johnson, M & J Outdoor Communications
Dwight Schuh, Sports Afield

STACKPOLE
BOOKS
Essex, Connecticut
Blue Ridge Summit, Pennsylvania

STACKPOLE BOOKS

An imprint of Globe Pequot, the trade division of
The Rowman & Littlefield Publishing Group, Inc.
4501 Forbes Blvd., Ste. 200
Lanham, MD 20706
www.rowman.com

Distributed by NATIONAL BOOK NETWORK

Second Printing 2008
Third Printing 2023, Stackpole Books

Book Design by Lydia M. Inglett

British Library Cataloguing in Publication Information available

Library of Congress Cataloging-in-Publication Data available

ISBN 978-0-8117-7247-1 (cloth : alk. paper)
ISBN 978-0-8117-7424-6 (ebook)

♾™ The paper used in this publication meets the minimum requirements
of American National Standard for Information Sciences—Permanence of
Paper for Printed Library Materials, ANSI/NISO Z39.48-1992.

To Delphie,
for her faithful moral support
and countless hours at the word processor.
And to the little sea geese,
with whom I've kept vigil on many's the lonely bay.

Second Printing 2008

Contents

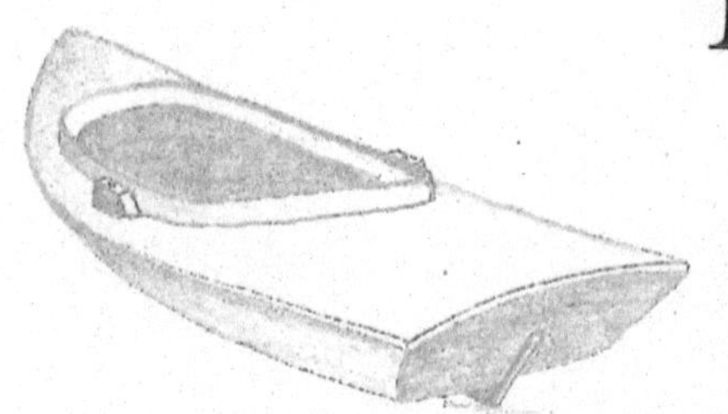

Foreword to the 2023 Edition

TODAY WE CALL THEM MENTORS. Back in the day they were simply called Old Men.

These were the men I grew up surrounded by. Steelworkers. Automakers. Shade tree mechanics. Carpenters. Disciplinarians. They were trappers, catching muskrat, mink, and coon each fall, skinning them in front of a woodstove.

And they hunted. Squirrels. Cottontails. Rooster pheasants. And ducks. First of the year would find them floating the East Branch of the Mahoning River, booted feet on either side of a charcoal-filled #3 coffee can, the gunwales of the 12-foot Sears aluminum semi-V white with frost. Sticking close to the inside turns; the still of the morning shattered by the startled *quacks* of red-leg mallards and blacks.

That was, for me, a long time ago, almost fifty years. I vividly remember my Old Men. And the things I learned, the places I went, the memories. Forged with a passion for the outdoors, a love of those winter red-legs, olive-billed black ducks, wide-water canvasbacks, green-wings, gadwall. Sprig and redheads. Strip off anything ornate and extraneous and you were left with but one basic element—a waterfowler.

And this was David Hagerbaumer, an Old Man, by my definition, not in years but truly in experience. At a level of "been there, done that" unmatched by very few exceptions today. Born in 1921 and growing up along the Mississippi River, he helped an uncle tend to a bevy of live decoys and showed a talent for trapping mink. He survived the 1940 Armistice Day storm, during which he narrowly missed joining the more than fifty 'fowlers who perished. There was a short-lived decoy business— Custom Bilt Decoys—that Hagerbaumer began with a cousin. In a stint as a US Marine Corps machine gunner on Midway Island, he downed a Japanese warplane, shooting it, as he recalled to colleague and fellow duck hunter Worth Mathewson, "as one would a drake mallard making a pass over the decoys."

Hagerbaumer left us in February of 2014, a loss to many. At 93, he had filled not only his world but the world of countless thousands with myriad two-dimensional flashbacks of things that only those who have awakened alongside a Washington tidal marsh or watched the sun fall while wrapped in an ages-old family stilt blind can fully understand.

I didn't have the opportunity to share a stretch of Willapa Bay with Hagerbaumer as he eagerly awaited another rendezvous with his wondrous black brant. Nor did I sit at the base of a springboard-notched cedar stump with him somewhere along the Oregon Coast, our eyes searching for the next flight of widgeon, with perhaps a drake pintail in the mix. I didn't have that good fortune. But what I did have—what I do have—are Hagerbaumer's visions. As do you.

Just open his remarkable work *Waterfowling These Past Fifty Years*—originally published by Worth Mathewson and his Oregon-based Sand Lake Press in 1998— and the journey begins.

Take, for instance, Hagerbaumer's sketch gracing page 100 titled *Abandoned Cannery at Oysterville*. I've been to that very spot . . . and listened to the long-ago sounds of the oystermen going about their day-to-day lives. In the background, we know courtesy of the chapter lead, lies Willapa Bay, one of the artist's most revered places. Home to his beloved black brant. To bluebills. And widgeon. And oysters . . . and to the ghosts of the rugged men and the courageous women who, with rake and skiff and determination, harvested Willapa's bounty throughout the mid-1800s and into the present. Hagerbaumer was there . . . to see the bay boom and fade and change and to capture in his renderings in *Fifty Years* the decoying widgeon and sprig, white-fronts, dusky Canadas, and canvasbacks.

You see it—the steam curling off the water in Hagerbaumer's world, this non-monochromatic universe somewhere between black and white. If you've been away from it for a while, there are men like David Hagerbaumer who, by way of the written word, paper, and pencil, pull us back into that which we and he know best. The marsh. The tides. The weathered wood. Wings. Whistles. Hagerbaumer's vision and his ability to take us to places seen and unseen live on between the covers. Let the artist and wordsmith reacquaint you, as he's done me, with the green-winged teal. The river otter. The rocketing snipe. The waterside shanty.

My notes would be incomplete without a discussion of the original publisher of *Fifty Years*, Worth Mathewson, himself a close friend of Hagerbaumer and a dedicated devotee of the waterfowling arts. I was introduced to Mathewson in the spring of 2021 by a mutual friend, Brad Bortner, former chief of the Migratory Bird Division, US Fish and Wildlife Service. But prior to that, I'd been introduced to Mathewson through his celebrated work, *Big December Canvasbacks*. I knew of the man's fondness for old side-by-sides, handcrafted decoys, scull boats, and gunning 'fowl internationally. He was and is, in the opinions of those who know him, the epitome of Old School.

In my first interview with Mathewson in June of that year, I learned much about the man, clinging, I came to realize, on each and every word. He killed his first duck, a Virginia black, in 1953 with a 20-gauge Stevens Fox double he'd gotten that morning for Christmas. Mathewson has ten books to his credit, has written for forty-three different magazines, and has hunted in ten countries, including Iceland and Siberia. On operating a punt gun in Northern Ireland, he recalled, "The gun was a double barrel shooting sixteen ounces of shot from each barrel. I made one shot of fifteen teal and widgeon."

Men like Worth Mathewson are the essence of traditional waterfowling. "I approached duck hunting," he told me, "like I did fly fishing. A classic approach. Flies instead of a gob of worms or a spinner. Duck hunting was similar. Hand-carved decoys. The gun had to have two barrels, side by side. That was mandatory for me. And, of course, the old boats. When I was a young man," he continued, "I was like any young duck hunter. I wanted to kill ducks. But as I grew older, it became less important to kill a lot of ducks versus just having a good day."

If you happen to be a waterfowler, *Fifty Years* belongs in your library. Though you might not have hunted the places Hagerbaumer writes of and though you may not know the waters of Willapa Bay, Humboldt Bay, or Washington's Skagit as intimately as he did, these are your places. The marshes and puddles, rivers and streams in the Carolinas, Ohio, Iowa, the Dakotas, and Texas. Hagerbaumer's world is everywhere, and it exists for all who have donned a set of waders, thrown a passed-down decoy, cradled a grandfather's first shotgun, or hugged a wet dog. Or will.

How to describe the visual significance of *Fifty Years*? Everything: from the watercolor pintails against a leaden sky on the jacket to river otters, black-necked stilts, gulls, barn swallows, a sand shrimp. And, of course, ducks, geese, cranes, and brant. Everything we 'fowlers see throughout the seasons or sometimes forget to see. It is a beautiful simplicity.

—M. D. Johnson
M & J Outdoor Communications / 2022

Foreword

I FIRST MET DAVID HAGERBAUMER AT ROCKY POINT, a small resort area on Upper Klamath Lake in southern Oregon. I'd grown up in that area and was hunting ducks with my old friend Don Hummel, himself an artist and an acquaintance of Hagerbaumer. Don told me Dave was hunting in the area and was staying in one of the cabins at the resort.

Sensing my excitement at learning David Hagerbaumer was prowling the same marshes we were, Don took me to Dave's cabin one night and introduced me to Dave. We spent several hours visiting with Dave, and two memories remain vivid in my mind. One was the coot stew. David Hagerbaumer, the famous waterfowl artist, the man enshrined for painting wood ducks and mallards, the man who had hunted every glamorous bird species across North America, had shot a mess of coots and was whipping up a fragrant stew from those humble birds.

"You know why people won't eat coots?" he growled as he breasted the coots for the stew. "They won't eat anything their mothers didn't feed them before they were seven years old." Right off I could see this was a pretty down-to-earth guy. My kind of guy.

The other point I remember about the night was asking David Hagerbaumer if I could write a story about him. You see, I was an aspiring outdoor writer, a beginner. At my level, I had no business even thinking of writing about a man of Hagerbaumer's stature. But as the evening progressed, his blue-collar, unpretentious talk about duck hunting put me at such ease, I mustered the courage to ask. On the spot he invited me to meet him on the Oregon Coast for a few days of hunting. We could shoot some ducks and get some pictures and put the story together there. The resultant story, "Hunting with Hagerbaumer," appeared in *Outdoor Life* magazine and proved to be a major step in my writing career. Dave has generously helped many people like me, particularly artists, get started.

When we met Dave on the Coast to hunt, I learned the meaning of enthusiasm. As we prepared for the hunt, Dave, who was about 60 years old at the time, bustled through the driving rain from his decoy room to his duck boats not only with the exuberance of a kennel-fresh retriever but with equal energy. And all the while he was pointing out new projects, new boats he was building, new decoys he had designed, his in-progress brant blocks. And he bubbled with his plans for new paintings, new books, new projects.

He also taught me about the art of duck hunting. My version of hunting over decoys was to throw out a few muddy Plasti-Ducks. Not Hagerbaumer's. First we set out several dozen mallard, pintail and widgeon decoys Dave had carved and painted himself. To these we added coot decoys, gulls and a great blue heron. And as the tide changed, we moved the decoys regularly to keep just the right perspective. Truly his decoy setup was a work of art.

In the field, Dave always downplayed his hunting and shooting ability, as if he were a bit of a duffer who just enjoyed being out there. But I learned that was a bit of a facade. One time we were lying flat in layout boats on an open bay, surrounded by decoys, when a widgeon swung to Dave's right, a nearly impossible shot for a right-handed shooter. Suddenly, at the report of Dave's gun, the duck tumbled from the sky. Incredulous, I looked over at Dave to see how he'd done that. He had his gun mounted left handed. Over several hunting trips, I saw behind his humility to witness a very skilled hunter and shotgunner.

Perhaps what I've respected most about Dave has been his insistence on freelance hunting. As a preeminent artist, Dave has received many invitations to join elite, productive gun clubs with no competition and fast shooting. He has always declined because, at heart, he's a freelance hunter.

One highlight of my writing life was the privilege of writing *The Bottoms*, a biography of Dave's formative years in the 1930s near Quincy, Illinois, where he spent his boyhood prowling the Mississippi River bottoms and developing the heart of a naturalist, artist and hunter. This book, long since sold out, has become valuable among art and book collectors. Even above its monetary value, however, *The Bottoms* holds a valuable historical record and perspective on waterfowling. In *The Bottoms*, Dave's life bridges a bygone era of live decoys, baiting and market hunting, to the modern era of conservation and high ethical standards. Having made this transition personally, Dave is a living museum of waterfowling history and knowledge.

Even more fascinating is Dave's response to passing time. Many people, particularly hunters, die with change. When conditions change, when hunting isn't as good as it used to be, they quit. They can't make the transition. Not Dave Hagerbaumer. His rampant enthusiasm has not waned. No, he doesn't hang onto the old ways, he doesn't shoot cases of shells, turn a gun barrel red hot, stack ducks to the gunnel of a boat. But, as he shows you the decoys he's carving, the blinds he's building, the new duck boat he has designed, the paintings he has laid out—the coots bubbling in a savory stew —you know nothing has changed. You recognize a man with a true duck hunter's heart. Dave's accomplishments and accolades could fill many pages, but perhaps more meaningful would be simply to say here is a man who loves duck hunting.

Meet David Hagerbaumer.

—Dwight Schuh
Sports Afield, 1998

Some Musings From The Author/Artist

THIS BOOK IS NOT A LITERARY MASTERPIECE with flawlessly crafted phrases, impeccable sentence structuring and punctuation. Any competent editor could have done that for me, but it would not have sounded like Dave Hagerbaumer, man of few letters.

This book will not contain a wealth of earth shaking messages, expounding on controversial conservation issues, or other subjects beyond my expertise. I leave all of the above to those qualified to expound. Well, maybe now and then I do voice a meek opinion.

Very simply, the pages to follow will be a compilation of some of my experiences as a waterfowler since the end of World War II. My first days in the marsh date back to 1929. This book covers the time span of a tad over half a century and geographically the total of our Pacific Coast.

I do have the tendency to bounce around a bit from bay to bay and area to area and a wandering recall can be blamed.

I've never laid claim to the title of expert waterfowler in the technical sense. Aware of this, the "how to" in this book is either unintentional, or necessary as part of a tale. Most serious fowlers have their own ways to hunt anyway, so attempting to tutor these guys would be foolish. Plenty of good books and magazines on this subject do a fine job. I do claim to be an expert in the art of appreciating our waterfowl. Especially the black brant of the Pacific. A long while ago, I wrote "black brant symbolize all that is wild and free." I feel strongly still that of all our wildfowl this simple phrase fits brant the best.

The pursuit of this grand little goose has put me in the chosen environment of the species. A good share of the time, conditions usually were rough and the weather, in particular, even worse. I respect these hardy birds and give them my thanks for fifty years of pleasure. In train, the brant have brought me into excellent days with other species, in many special places.

As for the brant, I still take one or two each season. For me, this is plenty. No need this late in the game to assess the day's quality by a body count. There was a time—but no more. I now feel the same in regard to the ducks.

My hope is to bag a brant now and then—so long as I'm able. Also a few ducks along the way. I have always felt doing this is one of my few good habits!

—Dave Hagerbaumer
Burlington, Washington 1998

Acknowledgements

My sincere thank-you to the folks who have contributed information vital to the completion of this book.

Doctor Morrie Johnson and Bill Cameron, for their help with the history of the Samish Brant Club. Thanks also to the Club for being great hosts. Jerry Lomesdalen, for details on Samish Bay brant hunting from a stand.

Tony Breckenridge, for the answers to historical questions regarding the Edison Hunting Club.

Larry, Rucker, for permission to use his photos of Samish Brant decoys for drawing reference.

Cindy Lou of Coronado, our daughter, for her research on dates and laws as well as supplying pictures and maps, etc. regarding branting on San Diego Bay, past and present.

Bill Pinches of Arcata, California for sharing his up-to-date knowledge on present status of Northern California brant bays.

Worth Mathewson, for a lot of stuff. Keeping me focused, bolstering my ego, being patient, extending deadlines and agreeing to write on the status of his home state of Oregon's brant bays.

Mit Harlan, for his well written account on the history of the Dunlap Towing Company's brant floats.

Tom Newell, thirty year hunting crony, who had ready answers to my questions on dates, places and people's names. Many thanks, pal.

Tom Albrect and Steve Wohlwend, both members of the Samish Bay Sports Club, for their help with the history of this club and extensive tidal marsh.

The Dunlap Towing Company, for hosting time aboard their houseboat Wannigan and brant float for both Worth and me in gathering reference for this book.

Ron Gruber, for his help on British Columbia's brant hunting status.

Bruce McCormick, for his considerable effort in compiling the Washington State brant seasons from 1956 to 1998.

CHAPTER 1

The San Diego Period

IN JANUARY, 1946 I WAS IN SAN DIEGO, rather than my home state of Illinois. Fresh out of the USMC after four years of active service, I was sorta wandering aimlessly about the City, wondering which way to turn, or jump. For sure a couple of hundred bucks of mustering out pay wouldn't go far—even back then..Very shortly my cousin, Glenn Humphrey was also discharged from the USMC, and by chance we met to share our bewilderment over civilian life and exchange ideas for survival.

Just how or why we came up with the joint idea to start a decoy making business escapes me now. But start Custom Bilt Decoys we did. In an old double garage then owned by Glenn's landlord, Felix Lyons.

I made patterns for sprig, wigeon, mallard, canvasback, redhead and bluebills. All species commonly hunted in Southern California. Also, patterns for Canada geese. The large race as well as cacklers. And, of course, black brant. In fact, we used our brant pattern to double for the little cackling geese. As it turned out, we had more sales of the cacklers than the brant. At that time it wasn't known to us that a good many guys went to the Salton Sea region to hunt cacklers while very few hunted brant on San Diego Bay. As time went on, we got special orders for species we had not made patterns for. These were a swan or two, perhaps a half dozen or so white-fronted geese and a few cinnamon teal. None of these just mentioned, to my knowledge, have yet turned up in collections. More surprisingly is that no wigeon have shown up, and the wigeon is one we made quite a few of as the Salton Sea gunners got many of this species.

Glen got busy and designed a one stage copy lathe using odds and ends from a junk yard. A bicycle frame, an old car steering wheel, shafts and pulleys, an electric motor and a cutting bit made at a local machine shop. Glen could turn out a dozen or more bodies a day and I could carve heads at about the same rate using a cutting burr held in a quarter inch electric hand drill. Finish work was done with rasps and sandpaper. When we'd carved three or four dozen heads and bodies we would work together assembling the decoys with dowels and glue. Then again, as a team we

CUSTOM · BILT · BLUEBILL · BALSA · 1946

CUSTOM · BILT · WIDGEON · BALSA · 1946

CUSTOM · BILT · MALLARD · BALSA · 1946

CUSTOM · BILT · CANVASBACK · BALSA · 1946

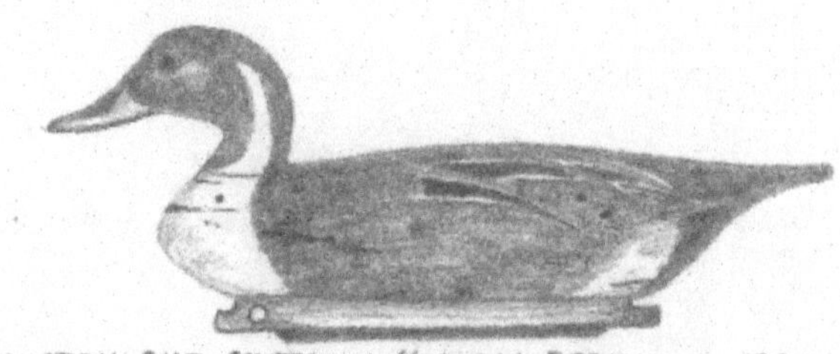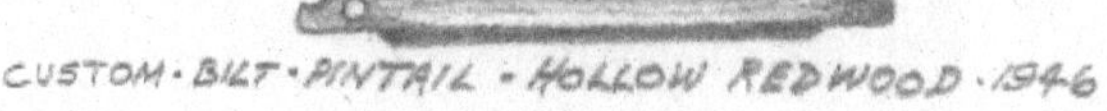

CUSTOM · BILT · PINTAIL · HOLLOW REDWOOD · 1946

CUSTOM BILT · WHITE · FRONTED GOOSE
BALSA - 1947

CUSTOM · BILT · BLACK BRANT · BALSA · 1946

CUSTOM · BILT · CACKLING GOOSE · BALSA · 1947

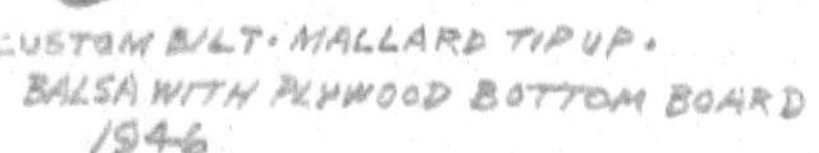

painted the lot. It went smoothly enough. Materials used were redwood and balsa for bodies and pine for heads.

As the year passed we made several hundred decoys. Most were sold at $3.00 per decoy, and we eked out a meager existence. Then came Fall, and the opening of the waterfowl season. It was finally a chance to test our products! South San Diego Bay was close at hand and in those years, much used by brant and several species of duck, and strangely, not many hunters.

During the summer, in addition to making decoys, we'd also built a Barnegat bay sneakbox. We used plans drawn by Edwin Megargee and sold by Field & Stream magazine. Unwisely, we substituted five eights marine plywood for the planking called for in Megargee's plans and as a result the hull weighed a ton! Hell for stout, though. But let me tell you that bending and securing that heavy plywood into compound curves was some task! In due course, however, we had a boat. And a Barnegat to boot. Here in the CBD shop my love for the time honored sneakbox began. Today, after more than half a century I still own and use one.

CUSTOM BILT · MALLARD · HOLLOW REDWOOD · 1946

CUSTOM BILT · CINNAMON TEAL · BALSA · 1947

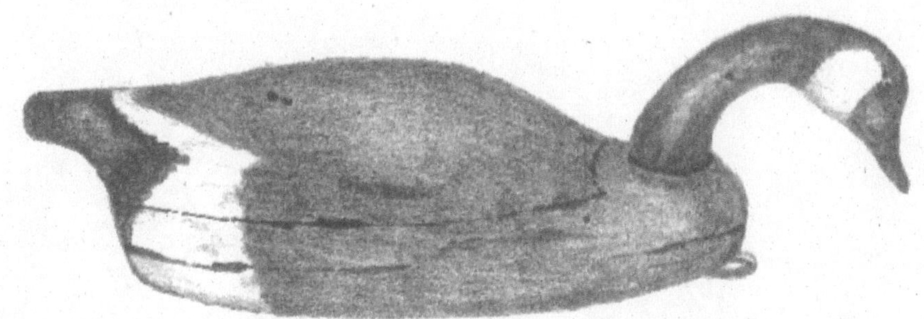

CUSTOM BILT · CANADA GOOSE · LAMINATED LIFE RAFT BALSA · 1946

Down in the Southwest corner of San Diego Bay, jutting out from the Strand was a point of land, maybe two-hundred yards long. Covered with salicornia "grass" and driftwood, it was THE logical land form from which to gun. Years before some other hardy wildfowler evidently thought so as well for a very sturdy pit blind adorned the point's extreme tip. Its age became evident when one examined the variety of corroding shotshell cases that littered the pit's bottom. Even some AJAX HEAVIES!

The Strand at that time was simply just a strip of sand that extended from the bay's south end northward to the town of Coronado—famous for its huge wooden hotel that operates yet today. A small naval base was also part of Coronado. The intervening seven miles of Strand, with the Pacific ocean on west beach and San Diego Bay on the East was barely a quarter mile wide anywhere along its length.

In the Pacific, off the Strand, stand the Coronado

AMERICAN WIGEON ♂

Islands. They lie about twelve miles offshore and are uninhabited by man. They do, however, provide habitat for many species of sea birds as well as seals and sea lions. In the surrounding waters, at least back in the forties, fishing was superlative. Yellowtail, white sea bass, black sea bass, mackerel, and many rockfish species were abundant. Charter boats made daily runs all year long out to the islands and now and then I splurged and bought a day's fishing. On one trip I won the "pot" with a black sea bass that was over a hundred pounds. The largest fish I've ever caught! As I think back on these fishing trips I'm not at all certain that just observing the wealth of bird life that nested, roosted on, and wheeled about the islands was not my main reason for taking these charter trips. The brown pelicans in particular

took my fancy the first time I met the Pacific ocean and still today to watch them dive for food is a never ending wonderment and fascination.

In the SW corner of the bay, the spit described earlier, jutted out into the bay. A nearby hog "ranch" prompted us to name the spit "Hog Ranch Point." If it had a previous name we were never aware of it. The small hog ranch was actually a feed lot, for here the owner fattened his porkers using cast off vegetables from San Diego markets. In those times, the brant season coincided with that for ducks. As a rule, ninety days long. Just what the wintering population of brant in San Diego bay numbered I cannot say, but there were plenty for good hunting I can assure you. They seemed to favor the bay's South end. I'd guess for better food source. Across the bay from Hog Ranch Point was the "salt works". Here The Western Salt Company had constructed a series of evaporation ponds from which salt was collected for commercial use. The salt piles showed up shiny and white on bright days from Hog Ranch Point a couple of miles away.

Duck and brant were gunned on the East shore near the salt works by locals, but never having hunted over there myself, I cannot vouch for the quality of the shooting. Hog Ranch Point and the little bay in it's elbow is where Glenn and I did our San Diego Bay waterfowling. We hunted together now and then but most often, I gunned alone, a practice I still savor.

To rig for brant from the point's pit blind, we'd unload the sneakbox from the roof of my '39 Plymouth. Fill her with CBD brant and sprig decoys and one would row out to the blind. The other would trudge from the primitive launch site over the drift logs and salicornia to the pit, thus lessening the load for the

BLACK-FOOTED ALBATROSS

oarsman. Once at the pit, the boatman set the rig of decoys while the walker tidied up the pit. This entailed removal of debris deposited by high tides as well as a lot of bailing of water. Let me say here that not always did we go blithely out to the pit and set up. This, after all was a public domain and now and then another party was there before us. No problem, however, as once we learned this fact of life we came prepared for another set up close at hand.

In the trunk of my Plymouth were several sacks of CBD bluebills. Here in the small bay behind the point, was to be had state of the art scaup gunning. We'd rig fifty or more decoys in a "fat" line and anchor the sneakbox parallel to the spread. We'd sit back-to-back in the boat. One would take incomers and the other outgoers. Maybe not very conventional, but it sur'en hell worked! Once during the hunt we'd change seating for variety of shots. Good times those! On a day that we found the pit vacant our procedure never varied. We had chosen a falling tide to be there. Not that tidal variations down there were that severe. Anyhow, a falling tide seemed, at least to us, the prime time to gun Hog Ranch Point.

Thirty or so brant decoys and half that number of sprig were rigged on the upbay side of the point. On a good day the action would be memorable. On others, only so, so. Always on Hog Ranch Point the outing was worthwhile. Solitude, a great variety of bay life to observe if nothing else, and now and then an unexpected meeting with another "hunter." One morning, as I came ashore at the base of the

CORONADO ISLANDS

point, I saw a fellow shooting at "shags" as they came over the Strand into the bay. I approached him and inquired as to his luck. He replied, "these brant are sure gonna' taste good roasted." I've often wondered through the years how that kitchen must have smelled as those cormorants were cooking!

One memorable day in the pit blind on Hog Ranch Point will stand out in my recall forever. Perhaps as vividly as a few others that I've experienced of the magnitude of Armistice Day Storm on the Mississippi 1940, the Newport Blow 1964, or the Netarts "Wind" 1972. I headed off along to the bay that day in the winter of 1947 with winds steady out of the SW at forty, I'd guess, and of course, heftier gusts that accompany all blows. As I drove toward South Bay feeling the old Plymouth shudder as gusts buffeted her I thanked my lucky stars that the point was in the somewhat protected bay there under the lee of the Hog Ranch. The short row out to the point would be no risky business in a Barnegat. Once at the spit and out of the car, the force of the wind began to really impress me. Glassing the point to make certain the pit was unoccupied, the chore of unloading the boat, getting it to the water, loading decoys and other gear began. As I worked, it seemed that the blow was increasing. Still no cause for concern it seemed.

Rowing out along the spit's southerly shore was uneventful and except for some slop over the after deck from following seas, the short haul to the pit was a snap. Once at the point, I pulled around the point's northerly shoreline and found the waters a lot calmer. With the wind out of the SW and the spit lying exactly E and W proved to be a great aid in rigging the stool. As I rowed about setting the usual thirty or so brant decoys and a handful of sprig I began to see

some bird movement. In fact, before I'd finished the set, brant decoyed on two or three occasions. One small band even landed among the rig. This was going to be some hunt—I just knew!

Not only brant were awing but also most of the other species almost always seen on the bay's south end. Lots of bluebills were about, which prompted me to consider going back to the car to get the blue bill decoys I always carried in the trunk. On consideration the thought of bucking those waves back to the car quickly put the quietus on that notion. If bluebills didn't want to toll to sprig and brant decoys—the hell with them. Once the blocks were set I ran the sneakbox up on the point and threw some grass and other loose flotsam over her. Now in the pit blind I really took time to assess the situation in depth with some total consideration—mostly regarding the elements.

In the first place, the wind was on the back of my neck and slightly to the right. Perfect, of course, except that to retrieve downed birds out in front of the blind would be a real chore. The wind would be blowing them out into the bay and that water out there was a churning mass of white horses! There was only one sane way of handling this hunt and very simply I'd shoot only birds decoying in on the north side of the point. They'd have to be coming in to the decoys cross wind and over the decoys. Once dropped there in the rig I'd have no problem retrieving them.

Very shortly, I had my first chance to test this plan. A handful of bluebills came downwind, almost over the pit, and made a wide swing to their left and rounded up right over the blocks. Can't recall now how I did, but there was at least one down in the decoys and in short order I had it in the boat and a bit later was in the pit again.

There were many brant flying around acting sort of goofy-like. But then, brant, God love 'em, can be like that. My theory on their behavior that day was this: The storm had driven a lot of them in from off the ocean and now once over the bay waters, they saw little improvement in water conditions and were baffled. Maybe even wondering why in the devil they bothered to leave the ocean in the first place. Brant can ride out "hellacious" storms afloat so I doubt they really needed to leave the ocean off the Strand in the first place. In time, brant did decoy to me and three were finally brought to bag by carefully following my rule of waiting until they were over the decoys.

By now I'd seen no sprig which was a puzzlement as Hog Ranch Point was almost always a sure fire pintail show. I like to surmise that sprig are so wise that they read the previous day's weather report and had done so the afternoon before, then "hiked" over the hill to nearby Otay Lake and right at this moment floated about on a serene surface. Not one pintail did I see that entire hunt.

The little scaup were still about and now and then one or a small bundle would decoy in just the right way and I'd maybe get one. In time I had a bag of bluebills as well as the sea geese.

All through the hunt I'd been dreading that row back to the Plymouth. I had hoped against hope to see the wind lessen or better yet, lay flat. As I sat there in the pit screwing up courage to get at it, a little band of bluebills rounded up over the decoys. Still below the duck limit I picked a drake and knocked him down. A cripple, and a lively one at that. Two more shots from the old Browning and the little bill is still a cripple and heading out toward heavy water. By the time I got to the boat and rowed out to the wild stuff the bluebill was nowhere in sight and even if I could have followed I knew from years of experience he was a lost bird. Alone and concentrating on the boat handling to stay afloat I quickly made the decision to abandon that bird. So far, the only sad note to a great hunt. Losing that duck took the spirit for the hunt out of me so I put my gear aboard the sneakbox, picked up the blocks and took stock of my situation.

The sneakbox was carrying three hundred pounds of body and gear and as a result did not respond to the oars so well as I would'a liked under the present sea conditions. Where the car was parked the spit was much wider, at least a hundred yards. At once I decided that I'd much rather carry the decoys across that stretch to the car than to row them around the point and then into the blow back to the car.

Once I reached the Strand I unloaded the decoys, gun, shells etc. and again

rowed out to the point and sat there for a minute to psych up for the pull around and into those rollers. At least now with the sneakbox somewhat unburdened and more responsive to the oars I took courage. Spray shield up and fully secured, spare oar out and handy on the floorboards, life preserver handy, not another thing to do but get at it.Looking at those waves from the pit was one thing but as I rounded the point to see them at water level was another sort of view—awesome. But then, not the end of the earth. Heck, I'd seen worse on the Mississippi River. Particularly those of that Armistice Day Storm in 1940.

Here we go, eh? Once out in the stuff and headed into the rollers it didn't really seem half bad. As the bow snouted into each and every roller the water came surging over the deck and smashed into the spray shield and poured on past over the decking on either side of me. After a dozen of these I calmed down and once again reassured myself that this was the sort of situation that old Cap Seaman designed this craft to handle. And handle it we did, Megargee's SCAUP and me. In due course we scrunched onto the sand at the base of the spit—the old Plymouth only yards away. Much to do yet, lug the blocks and other gear over to the car, load the sneakbox on top, and lash it all down. What a day! Makes a guy wanna' live forever!

Somehow at first I overlooked Mission Bay. Sure, I knew it was there—even fished for sand dabs near the Pacific Beach bridge. But for whatever reason it never registered as a branting opportunity. I'll bet the reason was that South Bay was so damn good! By the season of '47/48 though, with Mission Bay so close at hand, it couldn't be overlooked any longer. Several little "crick-like" runoffs from high ground to the East ran under Hwy 101 and into the bay during the wet winter period. Here, as one drove along the highway brant and wigeon mostly were often to be seen happily engaged in these miniature deltas seeking whatever it was that they found only there where fresh and brackish Bay waters met.

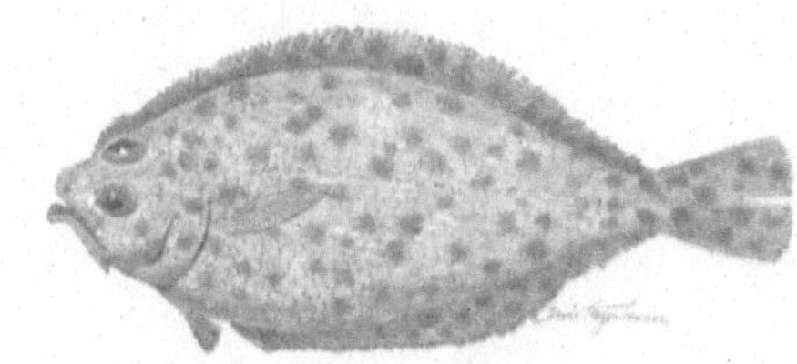

Very shortly I gave this bay a go for brant over decoys. The sneakbox was easily slid down the bank between road and bay. Decoys were rigged a ways out from one of the freshet deltas and the box grassed over for a layout mode. Strangely, though I tried this two or three times, I never connected with the brant or wigeon. In retrospect, my guess is that I simply never used the exact stage of the tide that the birds "used". Unknown to me then was the fact that Mission Bay was a GAME REFUGE. How I escaped apprehension is beyond me. But escape I did and lived free to hunt other waters.

An old timer told me that in the twenties there was a community of shacks out in the Bay's marsh off the delta of the San Diego River. These shacks were used by fishermen and waterfowlers of the region. In fact, he said there was at least one permanent resident in this little city called DUCKVILLE. This old coot, Ad Pearson by name, also held the title of "Mayor". As a permanent resident some of the temporary residents actually paid Ad a stipend to look after their shacks and trappings. It was said that Ad Pearson carved good working decoys and also painted oils. I never saw one of his decoys or a painting but later learned that what I've said is true. In any event, I did have some fun times on Mission Bay engaged in activities other than hunting. Fishing for sand dabs mostly. But also just "Huck Finning" about on a sunny day. The Bay's marshy cover was habitat for many species of birds, in particular, the sora rail, a favorite of mine. Also common were bitterns, wrens, blackbirds, herons and puddle ducks.

Here on Mission Bay, one Sunday a few years later, I made a monumental decision. At the time I was enrolled in San Diego State and just about to become an art teacher. As I sat there in my sneakbox, a fish line baited with sand shrimp in hand, the question came to mind for the umpteenth time, do I really want to teach? By now, after some practice teaching, I suspected this role was not fair to me, and of course, even more unfair to students to come. So, I made a hasty decision, one that to this day I recall and recount with great pride—I simply did not return to San Diego State the next day! So far as I know my locker there still contains my shoddy belongings!

That was Mission Bay in the nineteen forties. Now, I fear, it does not fare so well. A once almost pristine salt marsh and bay is unrecognizable as such. Convention centers, dredged up islands, motels, jet skis, water skiers, beach loungers, lounge lizards, and you name it—it's all there in decadent glory. The handful of acres left by developers and politicos--semi-unspoiled at the Bay's north

end (laughingly called a refuge) is stark testimonial to something that went awfully wrong! To add insult to injury, Hog Ranch Point on South San Diego Bay was forever lost, as developers covered it with an enormous housing complex about the same era as the Mission Bay debacle.

Glen and I struggled with CBD. Shortened seasons, and reduced bag limits were a burden for us. But mainly, we started a venture that was beyond our abilities as businessmen. Very simply we failed in the decoy business because we didn't know how in hell to market our product. We had a good experience and learned a bit about how it was "in the real world." No regrets. Glenn went up to Montana with his wife and did wheat farming, was elected sheriff, flew his own J-2 CUB and I am told is still living in Montana. As for me, I started my inexorable trek up coast for brighter horizons. Those that included brant, of course.

LEAST BITTERN

CHAPTER 2

Carson City

THE NEXT LANDFALL WAS CARSON CITY, NEVADA. A good friend, Tony Green, then director of the Nevada State Museum in this state capitol town offered me a position in that institution to prepare exhibits. Fancy sounding title that carried the not so fancy salary of three hundred dollars per month. It turned out that my job really was a jack of all trades. Collecting specimens for study skins and mounts, preparation of these specimens, work in the mine exhibit below the museum, and so on. As I think back on my times at this museum it was a great experience and a lot of fun. Tony and I were great friends, we hunted, traveled the state over several times in search of specimens, and actually made some permanent and worthwhile contributions to the museum's exhibits.

Major Max C. Fleischmann lived in Nevada and was an important benefactor of the Nevada State Museum as well as the Santa Barbara Museum of Natural History. Very quickly, once I'd met the Major, I became involved with the Santa Barbara Museum.

The first involvement was as a collector of specimens. It seems that the Museum in Santa Barbara was sadly lacking in goldeneye duck specimens. In both their study skin and systematic collections. I'd done some mink trapping along the Carson River nearby and was aware of the healthy wintering population of both species of goldeneye ducks along the stream's rocky gorges. Once I'd informed the

Major of this, the stage was set for some serious goldeneye duck collecting.

Tony and I worked as a team in this program. The river where the goldeneyes hung out ran through a series of gorges. Here and there along this course were short sections of slack water and eddies between longer stretches of turbulent current. It was simply not possible to get a boat into this section of the Carson River so it was imperative that the ducks be shot, killed, and dropped in these slack stretches of river so retrieval by wading was possible. Once perfected, our operation was simple enough. One man waited at a preferred slack water area and the other man drove the goldeneyes from upstream or downstream past the gunner. We eventually, over a period of a month or so, collected a total of around forty goldeneyes, and by judicious planning, lost very few specimens. A handful of these birds remained in the Nevada Museum's study collection and the remainder went to Santa Barbara.

The collecting of specimens for both museums took up a good share of my time and of Tony's as well. One day the two of us were in the pinon pine country not far from town looking for pinon jays. In the course of our search, Tony spotted an adult porcupine in a small pine. Tony was a great one for eating wild game so he just had to get that porky as a specimen—the hide to mount for a museum exhibit and the meat to eat. As I recall, someone had told him porkies were delicious. The truck was not far off, so Tony directed me to stand guard and keep the beastie treed while he went to the pickup to fetch a gunny sack. For some insane reason he wanted the "quill pig" alive! So, since Tony was, after all, my boss as Museum Director, I wisely let him call the shots. He was wearing a pair of very light weight driving gloves, so elected to hold the sack open while I swung the porky laden branch over the sack to shake him into it. As I attempted to perform my part of the operation

my misgivings mounted. In my mind the whole thing began to seem more and more like a Laurel and Hardie movie.

The harder I shook the tighter old Porky hung on. There came a point though when his grip slipped and down he came into the sack! Ah, success! However, all was not hunky dory, because as the thorny rodent fell past Tony's gloved hand he slapped out with his tail and very neatly pinned the fancy pigskin glove to that hand—just as effectively as if a staple gun had been used. So, back to the pickup we trudged, porky in sack and Tony's hand in glove. Once at the truck with a pair of pliers in hand I was able to remove a couple dozen quills from the glove and skin beneath and presto, the Museum Director was gloveless! As I think back on the episode, I cannot recall if Tony ever mentioned what porcupine tasted like.

In these same pinon pines "pine nuts" were also collected in the fall of the year. This is undoubtedly is one of the messiest jobs I've ever tackled. The nuts must be shaken loose from the cones by hand and in short order ones hands are so bound up with the cone's pitch that fingers must be forcefully separated with the other hand. There comes a point at which the build up of pitch must be removed with a solvent. We carried a gallon of kerosene for this purpose. Pine nuts are a taste treat but I've never had the urge to gather my own since. Take my word for it—whatever price you must pay for your pine nutmeats—they are a bargain.

While working in Nevada I bagged my first chukars and sage grouse. The State has a lot of habitat for these species and as I traveled over the entire State, mostly for the mine exhibit, the opportunities to hunt were just about endless.

The mine exhibit I keep referring to was a fun project. George Smith, a retired gold miner, was hired on, specifically for his knowledge of the old time mining

methods, and also for his experience in actually "building" mine shafts and tunnels. The where's and how's to cut and install lagging, lining and bracings of timbers, also how to lay narrow gauge track for ore cars. George knew this all from fifty years as a hard rock miner. We traveled the State together and gathered old rusted equipment, old timbering, track, ore cars—you name it, we found it. Some from long abandoned mines, some actually from old mines of George's as he held several claims he swore he'd reopen when gold rose in price. It was $32.00 an ounce at that time as I recall. Most likely some of George's claims would be very profitable today with gold pushing four hundred dollars!

We trucked back all of these goodies to the museum and stored in the side yard.

George and I labored side by side for almost two years building a model gold mine in the basement of the Museum. Ore car track was laid. Along the walls were exhibits showing the various techniques of mining from the late eighteen hundreds to the thirties. We used the timbering recovered from old mines and reinstalled it in our exhibits to duplicate exactly the way those old mine shafts and tunnels looked. The whole project turned out as hoped. The public loved it. In fact, the "mine" is still open to the public viewing there in Carson City under the old mint building which is the Nevada State Museum.

At one point in our excavating for an exhibit, we ran across a pocket of gold dust. George was baffled to find gold there under the Museum. After a good bit of sleuthing, old George figured it out. Originally this building was built as a U. S. Mint. Gold and silver were turned into coin of the realm here. We had found the little pocket of gold dust in the soil directly below where a washroom had been located when the building was a mint. Workers above had washed their hands for years and years. A flake of gold under a fingernail here and there was washed into the sink and down a drain pipe. Finally the old pipe simply rusted away and the gold flakes trapped in an elbow of the long gone pipe was recovered by us in the late forties.

During my employment at the Nevada State Museum I was "loaned" to the Santa Barbara Museum for collecting purposes. One of the areas used for much of the bird collecting over there on the coast was Morro Bay. The first time I saw Morro was in the winter, and of course, the bay was loaded with brant. That did it! From that moment on, I schemed with all of my might to get "transferred" from Carson City to Santa Barbara. Thanks to my good friend by then, Major Fleischmann, it took but a word or two from him and the deed was done. I bade fond adieu to Nevada and hiked my bones over to the Santa Barbara Museum of Natural History—and the salty air that smelled of sea geese!

CHAPTER 3

Santa Barbara

MY EMPLOYMENT WITH the Santa Barbara Museum of Natural History carried with it an even fancier title than that in Carson City. How about Staff Artist and Assistant Curator of Ornithology? Somehow I felt I had come up in the world, although my salary was still exactly that as in Carson City. Oh well, "it all counts on thirty" as I heard so often while a Marine. Again in Santa Barbara, as in Nevada, I liked my work, felt I was accomplishing something worthwhile in the building of museum dioramas, and my fellow workers were pleasant folks. My entire time at the Santa Barbara Museum was one of a satisfying nature.

Here again, in Santa Barbara a good deal of my time was spent helping in the collecting of specimens. Birds and mammals but also fish now as the museum was embarking on the task of building a Marine Hall. This collecting kept me in the field or under water and I was happiest out of doors then as now. Once at Santa Barbara, and on the coast again, my plans for hunting seasons were focused mostly on brant. The closest brant estuary was Morro Bay. A lot of our bird collecting centered about Morro and as a result I quickly made several good friends there, all of whom were waterfowlers. And one, Tom Tolman, a branter to boot. Tom held oyster bed leases in Morro Bay and when we were collecting bird species that frequented coastal waters, we mostly used Tom's properties in the bay. Memories of sitting on a bucket surrounded by millions of live oysters, shotgun across the knees ready to collect anything that flew by, and all the while killing time opening and eating oysters so fresh it made one whimper, are still fresh in mind. Knowing Tom Tolman ,who lived on property overlooking Morro Bay , gave me a leg up in learning the bay. He was invaluable consul in the selection of the most productive areas to rig out for brant.

Back in the forties and fifties a dedicated group of hunters targeted brant on Morro Bay. Most of this band were locals and all that I met were most knowledgeable and respected the sea goose as the trophy bird it is. A few sculled but the majority gunned over decoys—some from boats, some from shore blinds.

My first hunt at Morro Bay was on the south end along the fringe of the marsh. It was one of the areas that Tom had recommended. I used my sneakbox, of course, and the CBD brand decoys that I had pampered for a decade. This initial hunt was a success bag-wise but stands out in my mind as special because at one time during this hunt I was literally surrounded by brant as I lay concealed in my sneakbox. Birds started to come in to my area, the first ones decoying to my spread. Soon, as a bunch landed, more followed. Flock after flock came down bay and all kept adding to the growing brant on the waters. My puny spread was soon engulfed in the mass of gabbling birds. This went on for several minutes— not more than thirty. Then, no more flights. By this time, however, I was in the center of a flock of brant the likes of nothing I'd ever experienced before or since. I try to be conservative when I tell this story but it isn't easy. I swear there were five-thousand brant along that marshy shoreline. In front and on both sides of me and my decoys. I couldn't stay there forever so eventually stood up and those brant nearest me flew off, but not far. The mass of birds was still on that end of the bay when I gathered my decoys and rowed back to the boat launch. I can only guess as to why this happened. Tom Tolman and two or three other branters of the bay had no ready answer to my experience that day. My own theory is that I happened to be in the right place at the right time to see a migrational surge of brant. Flock after flock had come down the coast, turned into the bay at Morrow Rock and in half an hour all ended up on the water around me. It was something all right. In truth, other than brant, the water fowling possibilities around Santa Barbara were pretty slim. A new lake, Cachuma, just over the mountains from Santa Barbara, in the Santa Ynez valley, did offer marginal duck hunting but fisherman were so numerous that a quality hunt was difficult.

Up coast from Santa Barbara was a tiny estuary named Surf. Maybe there is a small town there. Surf shows on the map, but I never saw one. This small creek delta did have a few ducks from time to time and through the years while at the Museum I had several good hunts at Surf. All over decoys and from a shore blind.

My immediate "boss" was a great fellow. Twenty or more years my senior, Mr. Egmont Z. Rett, had made a career of museum preparatory work. He was one of the finest bird and small mammal taxidermists I've ever known. Trained earlier at the Denver Museum of Natural History, "Eck" had migrated to Santa Barbara in the late thirties. We hit it off at once and became the very best of friends. Waldo Abbott, the Superintendent of the Building and Grounds, also employed at the museum was one of the "three musketeers" we soon formed. We all loved to hunt and did so as a trio at every opportunity. It followed, of course, that we three formed the team that did ALL of the bird, mammal, and fish collecting for the Museum. As I think back on my Santa Barbara Museum years I am not at all certain that any of that time was work. Just about everything my job entailed was pure fun for me. Especially the collecting trips. I saw new habitat, built a modest knowledge of ornithology, and did all of this in company of my , by then, dear friends, Egmont and Waldo.

The Santa Barbara beaches were prime shorebird habitat in both spring and

SANDHILL CRANES DECOYING

HAGERBAUMER PROFILE DECOYS - MADE OF PRESSED BOARD - FOR COLLECTING SHORE BIRD SPECIMENS ALONG THE CALIF. COAST - 1950's -

fall. We did the bulk of our shorebird collecting on these beaches. I went one step further and added shorebird decoys to my efforts. Shorebird hunting was abolished in the twenties so having an opportunity to bag several of the species that were shot for the market a century ago was a thrill. And over decoys yet!

One collecting trip was somewhat unique. For some time, before I came on the scene, Eck and Waldo had been trying to collect enough sandhill cranes for a water hole diorama. They wanted at least eight birds for this scene. They had been trying to get these birds in an area up around Los Banos but with no success. After I was hired and the subject of cranes came up and I heard the negative results of their efforts I asked, "have you tried decoys?" With blank stares at one another the joint answer was, "no." In short order, under my direction, we had made a dozen or so silhouettes from fiberboard. Not a long lasting decoy but with proper treatment would do the job. A trip was arranged and in due course we were on the crane grounds in the San Joaquin valley. Some advance scouting revealed a water hole were the cranes watered in the afternoons. Next day by noon we were at the stock tank's where their overflow created the "water hole". Our shadows were set up, makeshift blinds were made from brush stacked alongside the stock tanks, and all to do now was wait. The cranes came, alright, in late afternoon and the shadows pulled them in like magic. In two days we collected the eight or ten specimens needed for the diorama. In one fell swoop I was given equal status as a team member.

Bird collecting was without a doubt my favorite task for the museum. When I joined the staff the museum had just entered a major expansion phase. Several benefactors, including Major Fleischmann, had made handsome grants of money, most of which had been earmarked for special projects by the donors. The Major, being an avid bird hunter was particularly anxious to see the Museum's study skin and systematic collections of birds enlarged. Very few species were well represented, so collecting meant pretty much anything that flew. There were exceptions, of course. No California condors, eagles, or trumpeter swans, for example. After all, there had to be limits. One of Major Fleischman's several hunting clubs scattered about the country was a pristine piece of creek bottom not far from Ventura, California. The size escapes me now but I'd guess it was several hundred acres. We collectors at the Museum had free run of the place except during duck season! One day, while collecting there, I tried a new form of wing shooting. With a smooth bore .22 I spent an afternoon shooting swallows with shot cartridges loaded with number 12 shot. This fine "bird" shot is referred to as dust shot. After some warming up I found it not that difficult to take swallows on the wing as they swooped about feeding on insects over the duck club's ponds. In fact, I also shot several common snipe with the .22 smooth bore on another trip. For those who consider the .410 the ultimate in shot gunning with a small bore—try the .22 smooth bore!

Being the loner that I've always been, there was seldom a time that Egmont or Waldo were a partner on my waterfowl hunts. Except at Surf. Here on this minus-

GREATER YELLOWLEGS

AMERICAN AVOCET

LESSER SANDHILL CRANE

LONG-BILLED DOWITCHER

HAGERBAUMER SANDHILL CRANE PROFILES.
PRESSED FIBREBOARD. USED IN 1950's
FOR COLLECTING SPECIMENS ON
THE PLAINS AROUND THE TULE ELK
RESERVE IN CALIF.

cule estuary we frequently all went to toss our dice as Surf was a crap shoot as a duck hunting spot. Surf was never, when I saw it, overrun with other gunners. When one was encountered that shooter was always exactly that—a shooter. A free soul that drove from damp spot to damp spot in the county hoping against hope he'd jump something with web feet. We, I suppose, overdid it at Surf so far as preparation for a hunt went. Mainly, of course, because it was I that insisted on decoys, a blind, and some traditional moves that at least suggested we were waterfowlers.

One hunt at Surf I recall well. The three of us, Egmont, Waldo, and I, had made some moderate preparations for this hunt. I had the decoys, mostly aged CBD's, but workable. No boat was needed at Surf so that left only the repair of our blind. It was a blind we had built along the willowed shoreline some years before. A typical coastal California morning (weather-wise) unfolded as we set a meager spread of tired and aging Custom Bilt mallards and sprig. At the time, there was no indication that another human was lurking about the estuary. As full light evolved it was evident that the musketeers were not alone. We were not in full command of the Surf Gun Club! There, just across that "vast" expanse of estuary waters loomed another hunter. This person, eighty or so yards away, on the far shore of the little bay appeared sorta clown-like. For there he (or it) sat out in plain view on the open shore on some sort of stool or box. This figure sat there with a gun across its lap. Just crouched there in a dejected sort of attitude as tho the situation was some form

of physical punishment. Surf was, as a rule, a sort of hit or miss affair duck-wise. In due course, a duck or ducks, I can't recall now, decoyed to our rig and as they did over this narrow estuary on one swing they were in range of this creature huddled over on the far shore. The troll came to life, stood up and blasted away at the birds. Again, I don't remember if any fowl were brought down, but one fact of life became very clear as the shots rained pellets all over and about us. Waldo was struck on the nose by one shot, hard enough to draw blood. A situation that at the onset was a little humorous quickly became very unfunny. Waldo, not know for his patience, erupted with a volley of swearing, all directed at the person across the water. This verbal abuse had no affect as the shooter simple sat down once again in the huddled posture. The morning wore on. We got a few birds, the parasite across the water got a couple, but eventually we three decided that the hunt lacked quality from the start and for sure wasn't going to improve, so we packed it in. As we headed for the car, the figure still sat huddled on its perch.

With premium waterfowling no closer than Morro Bay, some hundred plus miles to the north, I was not getting to do as much brant and duck hunting as my soul needed. Sure, today a hundred and twenty-five miles means little. Seventy mile speed limits, freeways with no slowdowns—these changes surely have "shortened" distances. With '39 Plymouth, two lane highways full of slow curves made for a combination to make a mile exactly that—a mile. To the point, I was getting antsy for quality wildfowling closer at hand.

A GOOD DAY AT SURF

During this unsettled period, I'd made several exploratory trips even further north than Morro Bay to two premier brant bays north of San Francisco. These would be Tomales and Bodega. The two are quite close together, only a short distance north of San Francisco. In the heyday of branting on the entire Pacific coast these bays held a reputation as high as any of the others. I made the long haul from Santa Barbara up to Bodega and Tomales a couple of times. Both trips were of several days duration so as to make the safari worthwhile and both times I had good luck on both bays. Tomales had several stilt blinds that were built and used by locals but Bodega had none. Here on Bodega the gunners I saw used shore and sand spit blinds. I, of course, used my old standby, the sneakbox, as a layout rig or grassed along shore.

Another estuary reputed to be a good one for brant was Drake's Bay, even closer to San Francisco. I looked it over but never hunted there as access to it was too restricted then to be worthwhile. Old records do speak in glowing terms of this bay as a branter's paradise. Now all these years later I sometimes fret because I did not go to the effort to hunt Drakes at least once.

Of the two bays, Bodega was my favorite. It had easier access and a "branter" feel. The lower land forms surrounding Bodega made for a more open feeling than Tomales. And, Bodega had some sand bars and good shoreline cover for the sneakbox use. However, both bays held good populations of brant. One of my Bodega hunts was a classic. It's one of those hunts I've nick-named as "text book." I'd chosen to rig up along a grassy edging on the bay's west side. About three or four hundred yards up bay there was a sand bar that appeared on an ebbing tide. The weather was perfect. Overcast and cold with a brisk wind from the south that would bring decoying birds into my rig from left to right and almost parallel to the shoreline. I was rigged by good light and the tide had dropped enough to expose

the sand bar mentioned earlier. Some brant were trading around by now but I'd had no action. As the bar up bay became more exposed I noticed a boat approaching it from the north. There was but one man aboard. Through my old binoculars, the boat showed to be a wooden skiff of about sixteen feet and simply loaded with decoys. The fellow pulled up on the bar and hastily started setting a lot of decoys. But along with the decoys were full bodied stake decoys. Not until a while later did I learn that the full bodied stake decoys were, in fact, the gunners floaters as well. He had simply drilled holes for a stake into the flat bottom of all of his floaters. Once at the bar he could grab any decoy and a stake knowing he had a bar decoy. No fooling around trying to keep one kind separate from another type. Very clever. This dude was a branter! In a while he had over a hundred decoys rigged. About half on the water along the bar, the rest on the bar between his low blind of brush and the water. Around his brush blind were ten or more oversize shadows.

While my friend on the bar was still setting out, I got some action and bagged a limit of brant in text book-fashion. Soon the sandbar gunner began to get shooting and he also was through almost before it began. As I watched him get his birds so easily the thought crossed my mind, as I bet it did his as well, "was the enormous task of setting all these decoys

worth it?" And, of course, I knew his answer would have been mine "you bet!" With but thirty plus decoys, it took me but a short time to pick up, so I rowed up bay to meet this fellow who was just getting started in his pick up. We visited a bit as he worked—I even gave him a hand for a bit. He was a local, hunted this bar most of the time as weather permitted, carved his own decoys, and had grown up on Bodega bay. As I recall his name was Sam or Stan, but I never got a last name.

As described earlier, his floaters were all alike and all had a hole in the bottom to accept a stake. They were heavy blocks, solid cedar or redwood. Not long ago, Worth Mathewson gave me a photo from his archives of Bodega Bay. This shot is

of a gunner standing on a sandbar next to a brushy blind surrounded by large shad-ows. Flat bottomed floater decoys stand on stakes between blind and water and many more float along the sand bar's edge. Some ninety plus decoys can be count-ed in this photo, which according to Worth was made circa 1950. Gunner and carver unknown. I cannot help but feel that this is a photo of Sam or Stan. It would be interesting and fun to sometime go back to Bodega and circulate around town with this picture just to see what could be learned.

At the time of this writing I've been a scatter gunner for sixty-eight years. All of this time I've favored the pursuit of waterfowl but have not spurned the upland species by any means. With this mentioned, let me say that during my Santa Barbara years I was party to the finest valley quail hunting of my life.

Eck had a pointer named Belle during those years. The McMillan brothers had given the dog to him as a pup. Belle had been injured early in life and had a slight limp that never seemed a hindrance when she hunted. Waldo's father was the foreman of one of the several large ranches that occupied the vast Santa Inez valley, most of which was prime quail habitat and band-tailed pigeon woods. With the influence of Waldo's dad, his ranch was open to us as well as a couple of others on a limited basis. Being one of the musketeers it was seldom that I was not included on the quail and pigeon hunts that the others hosted over in the Santa Inez. As I

think back on those years of somewhat lean waterfowling times, for me it was sure-ly a break to have such fine upland hunting. Egmont and Waldo were also good friends of the McMillan brothers up Shandon way. Both Ike and Ian were ranchers and had large holdings, which included a wealth of fine valley quail habitat. Icing on the cake was that the McMillans were dedicated quail hunters and great hosts. They each kept kennels of pointers and were generally regarded up in the Shandon neck of the woods as premier quail hunters and pioneers in valley quail manage-ment. It was my good fortune to be a guest on the McMillan ranches now and then. In company with Eck and or Waldo, of course. Some years were banner years for both quail as well as band-tails. But even in years of lower than average populations of either species the gunning was still excellent.

In the fifties, in this area of California that boasted some of the finest valley quail habitat anywhere, there were still coveys whose size were at least reminiscent of the good old days that the old timers told of. I had the good fortune to witness coveys of two hundred and more quail flush before Belle's point. This I've been told was a drop in the bucket when compared to what it once was. These same his-torians calmly tell of coveys that held hundreds of quail, perhaps upward to a thousand. But a covey of two-hundred plus boggled my mind.

For band-tails we hunted the vast oak forests over in the Santa Inez valley. One of this wild pigeon's favorite winter food in the Coast Range of California is the acorn. Some say this diet gives the flesh a bitter taste but for me it was a taste treat. Later on, up coast, when I hunted pigeons in the Coast Range of Oregon, I did find these birds to be of a milder flavor on their diet of elderberries. As a game bird, I must rate the band-tailed pigeon first rate. None better for my money. Sadly, today, this species seems to have fallen on hard times over most of its range. In some areas (like Washington) there is no season at all. The reason for the decline is cause for a good deal of speculation by gunners. What the scientific community has discov-ered I've not been able to learn.

In any event, my time in the museum had reached a point of termination. I'd been offered the directorship if I would only complete one short session in college to get my BS degree. This would have required only one Spring or Fall session, and the museum offered me leave of absence, payment of tuition as well as my salary while in school. Also, with the job as Director, was a large home on shaded and walled Museum grounds, rent free, grounds cared for by staff gardeners, and the home itself maintained by the building staff. All very flattering, of course, but an art career loomed on my horizon, my feet itched and the north wind called.

As for the art, I had begun attending outdoor art marts in San Diego, La Jolla, La Mesa, and in San Barbara as well. These were weekend affairs and in a very short time I earned more money at these than from my museum salary.

Also, at this time, a Mr. Selden Spaulding, then the head master of the Laguna Beach School of Hope Ranch in Santa Barbara, commissioned small paintings of native flowers and birds. Selden was acquainted with Ralph Terrel, Curator of the Crossroads of Sport in New York City, and put in a good word for me. After that I

SNIPE RETURNING TO THE MARSH

BAND-TAILED PIGEON AND
BLUE ELDERBERRY

began supplying the Crossroads with game bird models in ceramic. Selden had commissioned me to do all the quail of our country, so I simply made others for the Crossroads using the same molds I had made for the Spaulding's collection. In a short time Ralph Terrel suggested I send him some watercolors. This I did. These were small pieces that he sold for ten dollars each! I could not keep up with the demand so added larger and larger paintings at increased prices. This was my real start in the art business. In less than a decade from my start with the ten dollar miniatures at Crossroads, my dealer roster included the Sportsman's Gallery, Grand Central Station Gallery, and Abercrombie and Fitch. These were all in New York. In Baltimore I was represented by Purnell Galleries. In Chicago, by Von Lengerke and Antoine. In another decade after this I was represented by almost one hundred galleries throughout the country in both original paintings and prints.

My first limited edition print was published in 1964. A customer of the

Crossroads of Sport had bought s black duck painting of mine at a Duck's Unlimited auction and wanted to have a print edition made of it. He approached Ralph Terrell and the two men struck a deal. Ralph sent the painting to Frost and Reed of Bristol, England, and in due course, using the collotype method of printing, the firm produced an edition of 400 prints. All concerned were delighted with the results and for another four years, the Crossroads of Sport published one edition each year using Frost and Reed. I consider the black duck painting that the man bought at a D.U. auction as my most important piece in regard to attracting national attention. Things took off rapidly after that.

While looking to move, I had done some preliminary scouting up coast and found in Ashland, Oregon a taxidermy business for sale. An elderly Mr. Cummings was retiring and I came along at the right time. It was an old business, had a good roster of regular customers, and of greatest importance was a giant step north. True, Ashland was not on the coast but was within easy striking distance of Humboldt Bay for brant and about the same easy distance from that top of the line waterfowling region, the Klamath Basin to the East. With mixed emotions, I departed Santa Barbara.

BLACK BRANT

CHAPTER 4

Ashland

O NCE IN ASHLAND, with the taxidermy shop open and under control, I directed some time on the scout for duck and brant hunting. Brant on the coast, of course, and ducks over the Cascades in the Upper Klamath Lake area for starters. From Ashland the coast is roughly seventy plus miles away by car. Beautiful scenery through the Coast Range, but a tortuous drive over two lane roads. Quickly, I learned that the drive to the coast for brant on Humboldt Bay was no improvement over the Santa Barbara to Morro Bay trek. But, the scenery was a change and I was, after all, five or six hundred miles further north!

Humboldt Bay, very close to the northern border of California, is a brant bay with a long standing reputation as Premier. In fact, I believe Humboldt is one of the last bays in the state that is hunted for brant. Morro still is also, but on shaky ground as the anti-forces there have gained a strong foothold. Humboldt is one of California's largest estuaries. The area still very rural and the two towns on the bay, Eureka and Arcata, are supported mainly by lumbering and shipping. The bay is still one of the very few on the Pacific Coast where sculling is practiced. Branters on Humboldt scull, use layout rigs, hunt from shore blinds, and from stake or stilt blinds

The area is rich in decoy carving history and even today, many carvers still live and practice their craft in that region. A friend, Bill Pinches, is one of these craftsmen still carving and in my own personal brant rig there are ten or so Pinches blocks.

My old Megargee "Scaup" was still extant, but riddled with repairs and begging to be put down. But with a few more hunts in her, with some coddling, I continued to hunt mainly by boat whenever I could. The ice breaking hunt for me at Humboldt was about as typical as I could make it. I did not then know anyone who hunted waterfowl on Humboldt, so just tossed the dice and went over cold turkey. Having driven by the Bay a time or two and done some glassing I knew the North Bay had shore blinds on the west side and that South Bay had several stake blinds at the far end. This told me that brant used on the entire bay. So, for no real reason I chose to start on the north end and hunt layout.

In addition to my standard thirty brant decoys, I added a dozen sprig. This

BILL PINCHES - 1975
JIM STONE - PETALUMA
CIRCA 1960
PINCHES / BINGHAM   1960
JIM STONE
MAKER UNKNOWN - HUMBOLDT
BOTCHIE - HUMBOLDT - 1935
BILL WEBER - EUREKA
CIRCA 1955

brought back some memories of Hog Ranch Point where I'd started all of this branting nonsense. I like a brant-sprig combination, not because the two species consort, but because the sprig add a lot of white to the rig which, I feel, helps catch the brant's attention. Those fellows up on Vancouver Island, B.C. believed this as well. The Glover brothers told me some years ago, when they were still allowed to hunt brant, that some of the fellows along the east side of Comox and Qualicum Beach stretch, painted the white of their brant decoys with high gloss enamel. They swore that the shine of the white mimicked the shine of wet feathers. I sure won't knock this theory as no finer branters ever drew breath than those old boys up on Vancouver Island.

Should a guy be hunting brant where a lot of divers are present, a good combo of decoys is brant and cans and bluebills. Whatever duck species you use for this for be certain to use almost all drakes for best results. At the famous Humboldt Bay for my initial hunt for brant, I rigged my standard layout set-up. Brant and duck decoys in a "fat" line but with the duck decoys separated in their own cluster. The sneakbox anchored parallel to the decoy string. Shrimp netting over the boat and full bodied gull decoys on stakes on the gunwales of the boat. About six or eight. Kept the gull decoys separated as gulls stay out of reach of one another when perching. Picky, picky. I used an anchoring rig, with a black and white buoy, so when I needed to get going fast to retrieve, all it took was the release of one snap. If winds and tidal currents conflict, I used a single line with anchors at either end.

My first "go" on Humboldt was a snap. Almost as if I'd gunned there all of my life. Not only did I get into the brant, but duck action was good as well. Wigeon mostly. I had no quarrel with this, as the wigeon was my favorite duck. The shore blinds were doing a land office business my first day there, so I promised myself to try a grassed up hunt along that shoreline my next time over. This first day on Humboldt I saw also a couple of scullers. Fascinating for me to study these fellows through glasses as they plied their unique method of waterfowling. Deadly when done by the expert. I tried it for a while and never got the hang of it. Could barely get the boat to move—even in dead water! The only time I had a successful scull was on Willapa Bay later on.

Returning home from Humboldt, my mind raced. What I'd seen that first day there convinced me that this was a brant bay all right! Maybe I'd made a big mistake by not settling in Arcata or Eureka instead of Ashland? Yet, on the other hand, I liked duck hunting about as well as branting, so let well enough alone. In Ashland, I was between the best of both. Better than the deep blue sea, eh?

As time passed, I did a lot of exploring from my Ashland home base. Not only did I continue to hunt Humboldt for brant and ducks but my exploratory sorties took me up the Oregon coast as far as Florence. I learned that while there are several estuaries on the lower half of the Oregon coast, none provided quality branting.

From the Oregon border northward, no estuary has habitat and or conditions that would attract brant until one reaches Coos Bay. The next up coast is Winchester Bay (delta of the Umpqua River). Caught my first striper here. Both these estuaries are large. Being large, they had attracted big time shipping, log traffic and storage—the resulting industrial confusion. There were no brant in numbers worth pursuing. I like to dream that a century ago these bays teemed with brant, and maybe they did then, but in my time there it was a lost cause. On one trial hunt on Winchester Bay I took one brant but the effort was sans quality. I spent most

of the hunt dodging tug boats, towed log rafts and general commercial traffic. The confused bird that I took from a small band that did decoy was most likely as squirrelly as I was by that time. To my credit, I suppose, is that no bay was overlooked, nor tried in my efforts to explore the branting our Pacific coast had to offer.

While in Ashland, I had for a short time, an art gallery where I displayed my works. Ashland was, and is home to a thriving Shakespearean theater. One day a fellow came into the gallery to kill time between plays and I met Louie Gephart. He lived in Eureka, he said, and came to Ashland to see plays and hunt doves. " Did I hunt?" My answer cemented a dear friendship right then and there. Louie would come over to Ashland for the dove opener every year. We'd gun doves together for evening shoots in some prime watering/roosting areas I had privy to.

One Fall, Louie presented me with a sweet little Fox .410 double on the afternoon of our first hunt that season. I shot that gun well for many years. Up until the time, I guess, when reflexes faded, and the little gun lost it's deadliness.

Louie owned and operated a sporting goods store in Eureka. A sign out front said it all, "Steelhead Louies". Louie's reputation as an expert fly tier and fly fisherman drew customers to his store from near and far. The north coast is blessed with many streams, some like the Eel, Smith, and Mad, have national reputations as premier steelhead and salmon waters. Louie knew them all like the back of his hand. As a result, if you were on the north coast, had any interest in fly fishing, a stop then at Steelhead Louies was mandatory.

The trip from Ashland to Humboldt Bay was a good long haul, so I generally made my safari there a three-dayer. It was the better part of two day's driving and one full day on the bay for brant and ducks. Seldom did I not visit with the Gepharts for an evening on these trips.

When Louie came over to hunt he most always fetched along some fresh dungeness crab. He taught me how to cook them, dress them, and several fine ways to eat

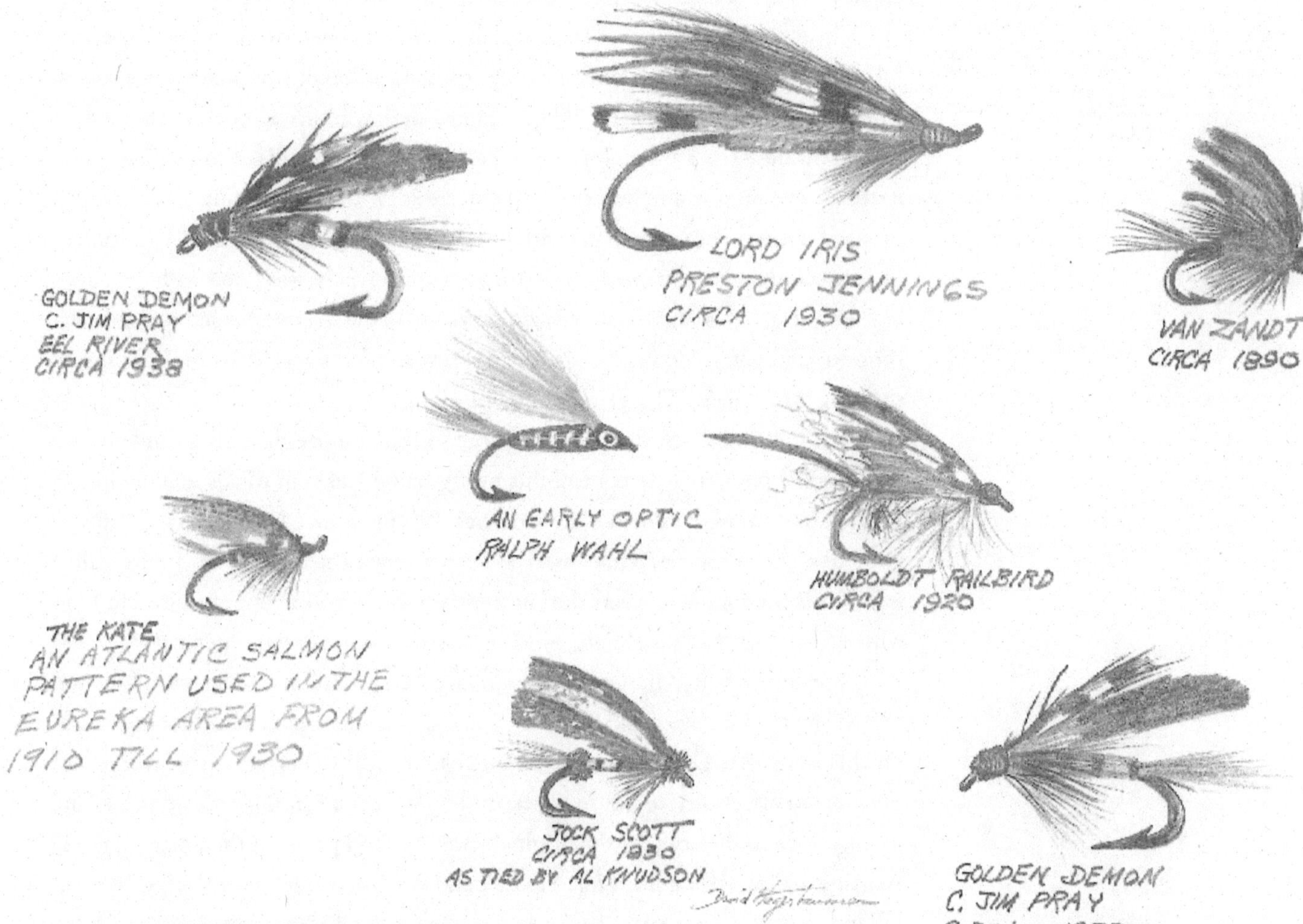

GOLDEN DEMON
C. JIM PRAY
EEL RIVER
CIRCA 1938

LORD IRIS
PRESTON JENNINGS
CIRCA 1930

VAN ZANDT
CIRCA 1890

AN EARLY OPTIC
RALPH WAHL

HUMBOLDT RAILBIRD
CIRCA 1920

THE KATE
AN ATLANTIC SALMON
PATTERN USED IN THE
EUREKA AREA FROM
1910 TILL 1930

JOCK SCOTT
CIRCA 1930
AS TIED BY AL KNUDSON

GOLDEN DEMON
C. JIM PRAY
CIRCA 1938

SOME OLDER STEELHEAD FLIES
OF THE NORTHWEST COAST

STEELHEAD TROUT

BLACK-TAIL DEER - FULL SHOULDER MOUNT

them. After this introduction and further upcoast, I taught myself to catch bay crab. Still today, my wife Delphie and I are avid crabbers, and eaters! In fact, I have an eighteen foot work skiff rigged specifically for crabbing, and for open water branting.

The taxidermy business, already established, was a breadwinner but demanded full time from me. With better income from art at hand, the smart move was to enlist help with the taxidermy. "Hap" Haptonstull, who lived close by was my first choice. Young Hap was employed at a local industry and in his off time often gravitated to my shop where he expressed sincere interest in becoming a taxidermist. First off, I hired Hap to help me with deer head mounting. A rapt and able student he grasped the procedures of taxidermy very quickly. He was good with his hands having worked as an upholsterer for some years. In due course, I sold my taxidermy shop to Hap and in doing so was free to exert my full energies to the painting of sporting art subjects. Things were moving along!

As a full time artist there was the urge to spend more time afield and amarsh for personal pleasures. To control this newly found freedom took some discipline. Fortunately I took command and won out. By this time I had started traveling a good deal gathering reference material from all over the country for future paintings. Over the following years during these travels I had the opportunities to hunt with several of my artist friends, which up until then, were only "pen pals."

One stop was in Minnesota where Dave Maass, Bill Webster, John Dill, and myself spent a long weekend hunting grouse and woodcock in Pine County. It was on this hunt that Dave Maass and I suggested to Bill Webster that he consider opening an art gallery to house his expanding collection of duck stamp prints and to introduce to the country the original paintings and prints of the up and coming sporting artists of that era. This, Bill did, and very promptly Wild Wings, Inc. was off and running! This year (1998) they celebrate their 30th anniversary and I will be represented by a grouse painting that I shall do shortly using the birch woods of Pine County as habitat.

On this same trip I met Chet Reneson of Lyme, Connecticut. As guests of one of Chet's friends, we traveled to Chincoteague, Virginia to hunt clapper rails. Our guide was Carlton "Cork" McGee. Cork is about my age and back there in the seventies was in his prime. Cork, by his own definition is a "waterman". This meant his vocation was fishing, clamming, guiding hunters, and all other related activities. This rail hunt was to be a two "dayer". We had all agreed that we'd shoot 410 guns, and as the weather was warm, tennis shoes would substitute for waders.

Cork had chosen two days of very high tides, reaching their peaks midday to early afternoon. The east coast rail hunting which I'd read about was done from a special skiff designed for that purpose, with the gunner seated in the bow and the guide poling the boat from the stern, as depicted in many famous sporting printings done in the late 1800s. Cork did things differently, and as it turned out, very successfully. I no longer remember the daily limit on clapper rail back then, but it was generous—that I do remember.

Cork's method was simple. The five of us were transported via his

"Chincoteague Scow" to a rail area of his choosing. The scow was anchored and we all got out and waded in a line abreast about thirty yards apart. The rising water forced the rails to little islands of higher ground. We even flushed some from duck blinds where they had taken refuge from the tide. Rails can swim, mind you, it is just that they choose not to. They can even dive when hard pressed. Cork caught several young ones by hand as we progressed through the flooded marsh grasses.

And so it went for two memorable days. The 410s were a great gauge for this hunting. The shots were close, we shot from solid footing, and so far as I am concerned, a larger gauge gun would not have been an advantage. I personally shot 3 inch shells loaded with 7½ shot from my Winchester Model 42. Chet, as I remember, also shot his Model 42 with the same shells. At one point I stumbled on a terrapin which Cork suggested that I keep. I carried it along in my hunting coat's game bag, and later deposited it in Cork's turtle pen at his home. For you see, as a waterman, Cork also caught terrapins for the commercial market. He told me the specimen I'd found was as large as he'd ever seem. I guess on the Baltimore restaurant menus of the old days, terrapin was as famed a food as the canvasback duck.

When the two day hunt for clapper rail was over, our total bag for five gunners was something just over seventy birds. Cork allowed as how this was not too shabby. On our last afternoon Cork took us to visit his long time decoy carver friend "Cigar" Daisy. His shop held all the mystic I'd hoped for. A great finale to a wonderful hunt. Cork and I stay in touch to this day.

I followed Chet back up to his home in Lyme and the next day he poled me about a small local marsh for sora rail. His skiff was of the design used from day one for rail hunting. To make this hunt with Chet even more special, it was one of the marshes on which Ogden Pleissner shot rails. When I would drop a sora, Chet would throw a child's football as close to the spot where the bird fell as possible. The plastic ball had been painted a bright orange and could be easily spotted. Birds were found easily using this method. I'm sure they would have been lost otherwise. The first night back in Lyme, Chet's wife, Penny, prepared a superb meal with some of the rails as the piece de resistance. What a memorable way to end my time in the Northeast.

About the time Leigh Perkins bought the Orvis Comapny I started painting sporting scenes for their gallery in Manchester, Vermont. Before long, I coaxed Leigh to work a blue grouse hunt into his busy hunting and fishing schedule—one which takes him to all parts of the world.

I'd been hunting blue and ruffed grouse in the Blue Mountains of north eastern Oregon for years with a long time crony, Vic Coggins, of Enterprise. Vic is a biologist for the Oregon Department of Fish and Wildlife, and knows every rock, nook, and cranny up there in the "Switzerland" of Oregon. These blue and ruffed grouse hunts were early in September, and seasons on valley quail and chukar were still closed at that time frame. It took a lot of will power while grouse hunting to ignore the flushing of quail and chukar as one moved through the coverts.

Another pal, Jay Long, a professor at Oregon State University in Corvallis, accompanied me on the trip with Leigh Perkins. Leigh had never bagged blue grouse, so when on the morning of the first day, as we drove up a logging road into the mountains, and three blue grouse ran across, Vic stopped the rig and suggested to Leigh to get out, load up his Winchester 21 and try them. Shortly we heard two shots from the timber, and then saw Leigh coming back down slope carrying a brace of blues. What a coup! A double on the first blue grouse he'd ever seen. A great way to start of three day grouse hunt.

Another remembrance of that trip was the pre-dawn breakfast at a local café after a bit too much celebrating at Vic's the evening before. As I sat solemnly in the booth opposite Jay, my thoughts ranged from why did I do it, to can I ever face food again. About the time I'd decided that any food that morning was simply out of the question, Jay calmly asked the waitress to bring him one raw egg in a glass of milk. The thought of it almost did me in, but was no match for the actual sight of it. To make matters worse, Jay sat there toying with and rotating the damned glass. As it revolved, the egg would appear and disappear only to show again like some sort of giant and evil yellow eye drowned in foamy sewage. To this day, I feel it is to my credit that I was able to sit through that breakfast hour toying with a single cup of black coffee and dreading the moment that Jay would slurp down that blasted egg!

Yet another incident from that trip comes to mind. At one point as we retrieved a bird, Leigh asked "doesn't anyone hunt with dogs out here"? I replied that a few did, and that Vic did most of the time. We would have been using his fine dog on this hunt, but unfortunately the fox terrier was at the Vet's with a stomach ailment. And that we had considered using his three lion hounds, but felt they were simply too hard mouthed to be of much use. Leigh looked at me long and hard, knowing full well he was being "leg pulled", but let the matter slide. Of course he knew—you see, he knew me!

The years certainly have slid by, I grew older, and the sideslopes steeper, and as a result, my Septembers with Vic in the Walloowas stopped. However, we still stay in touch.

The Ashland years were good ones. An art career appeared a sure thing and an income from it gave me confidence to make yet another move northward, nearer yet to the best brant bays that still survived on the Pacific Coast.

CHAPTER 5

Independence

Iɴ sʜᴏʀᴛ ᴏʀᴅᴇʀ I found myself in Corvallis, Oregon. A small, clean, and friendly city that boasted Oregon State University as a major reason for "being." After but a brief stay in Corvallis, I saw greener pastures some twenty miles north on the Luckimute River near the village of Buena Vista which stood on a bluff above the Willamette River. "Bueny", as the natives called the town, boasted of the last free ferry in the State. So far as I know, it still runs—capacity one large truck or wagon, or two or three cars, depending on size.

Three miles from Bueny was a farm of one-hundred and fifty acres for sale. Mostly bottomland, but also boasting one hill crowned with fir trees. This hill was the highest point in Polk County—according to the contour maps I saw at the courthouse. Over half a mile of Luckiamute River bordered the farm on three sides and provided irrigation water for the raising of hay—the sole crop of the farm. The "Lucky" a local name for the Luckiamute River was also filled with a giant race of

native crawdads. I still have the largest one I trapped mounted on a plaque—ten inches long, weight, seven and one-half ounces.

This was a great area in those years. Farms, creeks, rivers—serenity. A mailing address of Independence, Oregon was worth shouting about. Self employed, a steady income of substance, and ample time to savor all the waterfowling this region offered.

Just before leaving Ashland, time was at hand to face a dreaded chore. In packing to move north, the decision had to be made whether or not to move the "Scaup" one more time. Her ribs were broken and repaired over and over. The patches on her hull were quilt-like in number. With a solemn ceremony , I put the old girl to rest in a funeral pyre out there in the pasture behind the taxidermy shop. Now in Independence, I was "sneakboxless"! I've long lived by priorities, so immediately set to work and in short order had "Scaup II". "From the original Megargee plans? You bet !"

About this same time I became aware of fiberglass sneakboxes offered by two builders on the East coast near the original design's birthplace—circa 1836. They were Tom Pryor of Island Park, New York and Bill Kennebeck of Highlands, New Jersey. Both offered good looking hulls and after specs and photos were sent and studied I bought one from each of the builders. Now with three Barnegats I was awash with duck boats.

With a shop at my disposal once again, I immediately set to work on a new hand made brant rig. The CBD's had mostly been given away or worked to death. My goal was a rig of fifty shadows, a dozen or so hollow full-bodied, cedar stake-out decoys, and three dozen high density balsa full-bodied floaters. An ambitious project and one that would take some time. Time, I had, but patience I had not—I needed decoys now! The shadows were easy. Fifty could be turned out almost overnight. The full bodied, not so casually. To get going, I worked up the shadows at once. Now what to do about the rest? Brant season was not far off.

By chance, I saw an ad in an outdoor magazine for Otter decoys, made in Mediapolis, Iowa. They were advertised as heavy-duty foam construction. I ordered a snow goose sample and once in hand I figured it would substitute fine for a brant when repainted. The company was contacted and agreed to sell me unpainted snow goose decoys. The order for four dozen was quickly delivered and almost as quickly painted as black brant. Good decoys they were. Sturdy, oversize, and as it turned out, drew brant as well as any decoy could. Now I was set, at least for the first season on new branting grounds. As time passed I could work on the remainder of my dream rig as I could get to it. And I did.

To use a rig of this size a guy would need a sneakbox at least eighteen feet long! This dilemma was solved after some searching through magazines which turned up a double ender called the Li'l Ducker, mfg. in Minnesota. Made of fiberglass it was very light, twelve feet long. The Ducker seemed to be the "decoy skiff" needed. Once I had the Ducker and had used it under all conditions I was certain it was a good choice. In use, the Ducker was packed with decoys—under both decks, and

LUCKIAMUTE R. CRAWDAD

GREEN-WING DRAKE

OTTER FOAM DECOY
CIRCA 1978

SOLID CEDAR - OREGON COAST
MAKER UNKNOWN - CIRCA 1930

the cockpit rounded up full. Then, shrimp netting put over the cock pit and lashed down. The Ducker was then ready to be towed behind a sneakbox and if seas should capsize her, so be it, she wouldn't sink. And capsize she did once during a hairy blow up on Netarts. More about that later.

Back on the farm it became apparent quite soon that to run a hay farm, keep up with a building art career, and spend some time pursuing fowl was too much to fit into any one day. Priorities are priorities, so the hay farm was leased out to a nearby rancher who took it over, lock, stock and barrel—irrigation, cutting, baling, and hauling. The lease money paid the taxes, kept the farm looking good, and gave me breathing space.

My lease with the rancher did not include a twenty acre parcel near the river. It was not in hay and had a natural depression in the center. Another local farmer agreed to plow this piece every spring, I then planted corn and millet. A pair of tractors, a seed drill, a disc and harrow were included with the farm purchase. After the plowing was done it was actually fun each spring to work the ground and plant it. When the fall rains started the three acre depression quickly flooded the millet, leaving a small lake within a seventeen acre corn field. This of course, was an offering no puddle duck could refuse! As pat as this set-up was for bagging ducks I always felt

some guilt when I hunted my own private "duck club". The government says it is illegal to attract ducks by scatter feeding and then shoot them, but to plant the same feed, flood it and then shoot the birds, is not. When I asked why, no one was able to answer this question to my satisfaction. The practice still goes on to this day.

After a couple of seasons I stopped the practice of planting. I still hunted the farm's sloughs, a small lake and the depression on the twenty acres. The guilt faded as now the hunt was just that—a hunt. Not "luring the lamb to slaughter." As handy as the farm waters were they did not provide an intangible something that I found only on the river, coastal estuaries, or other areas that were "unfenced".

I've never been an avid hunter of big game. Once in awhile I shot a deer, just to have some venison and had about given up beating the brush for deer when the farm came into my keep. The Willamette Valley then had a black-tailed deer population that rivaled the cottontail rabbits in numbers. Well, almost. A biologist once told me, "we could put a bounty on the black-tails here in this valley habitat and not hurt the population!" A wild statement, sure, but not too far off.

On the farm, the undergrowth around the sloughs and along the river was almost impenetrable. The deer thrived with this escape cover and agricultural lands nearby for food. With venison so plentiful and handy I started shooting deer.

I found a rifle a hindrance so bought a slug barrel for my Auto-Five. This was venison beyond compare. The animals fed mainly on alfalfa, peas, beans, etc. in adjacent fields. None of that sage taste was there so noticeable from animals east of the mountains, nor that "goatie" flavor of coastal deer. The farm deer got me going again and every year I harvested a spike buck. No trophy animals! This fella was after prime venison. Since I sold the farm I've never hunted deer again.

Shortly before purchase of the farm I bought a seven month old golden bitch. Lady was a natural hunter and retriever and we hit it off at once. A field trial dog, "no"—a lady, and hunter, "yes". A better partner could never have been found. And she was in salt water while still almost a pup.

Up the coast was Netarts Bay. According to the research in Oregon Estuaries: "The 1857 General Land Office survey map of Netarts called it 'Oyster Bay'. Evidently, the large oyster population must have impressed the early settlers of the area enough to influence the selection of the bay's name. Although the name did not prevail, oysters remained abundant until the 1930's when a destructive parasite was unintentionally introduced through seeding with a foreign oyster. Today, both native and cultivated oysters remain at insignificant levels because the parasite continues to infect the bay."

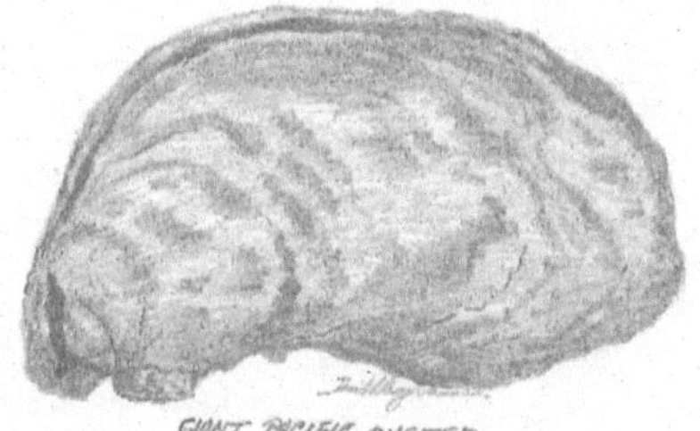
GIANT PACIFIC OYSTER

When I first started hunting on Netarts I would, at low tides, often see an oyster here and there. To find a few to take home to adorn a meal of roasted brant was always a treat. For me, Netarts was a jewel of an estuary on the same level of pristine quality as Alsea Bay on the mid-Oregon coast and Willapa Bay on the extreme Southwestern Corner of Washington. In all three bays, man's intrusion was minimal and they retained that untouched look.

Netarts ranks number six in size of Oregon's estuaries with 1500 acres of tidelands and a total area of 2300 acres. A narrow strand of sand dunes, grasses, and scrubby brush separate Netarts from the ocean along the entire length of the bay except at the north end where ocean and bay surge back and forth through a narrow gut, often referred to by the coastal folk as "the jaws". For me, the premier attraction of this bay was its wintering population of black brant.. Tillamook, ten miles up coast of Netarts also had a fine brant population. I've long felt that these two bays shared their brant numbers with frequent interchange. So, to say that one bay held more birds than the other would have been only a guess.

Netarts was the more enjoyable to hunt, if for no other reason than the solitude it afforded. This bay was not only top of the line for branting in those years, but also stood out with prime duck hunting. And, for icing on the cake, there were then only a few hunters. These were mostly local regulars, who, were for the most part, experienced and dedicated gunners. They were gunners who respected the right of others to enjoy a quality hunt. While living in Independence I'd surmise that ninety percent of my branting took place at Netarts Bay. The other ten percent at Tillamook and Yaquina. In recall, Netarts remains one of my all time favorite branting estuaries.

Frequently during a season Lady and I would overnight at Netarts for brant

and duck. This involved one of the sneakboxes and since the two of us would sleep in the boat, my choice was always the Bill Kennebeck model which had more roominess below decks. I'd pick a pair of days with a low tide in early morning. This way I didn't have to start out on the long drive to the coast so blamed early. Most often I'd launch in Whiskey Creek as the haul from there over across the bay to the section of strand I liked best to hunt was only a fraction of the distance from the public launch at the head of the bay near town. If the weather was calm this was no big deal to travel some further, but when things were lumpy, believe me " pardner," it could be desperately important.

Once at the strand, decoys were rigged, the sneakbox grassed-over alongside the cutbank that formed the edging of the bay along this portion of the strand. Salicornia "grass" grew in profusion here and this along with eelgrass piled in windrows by high tides made blinding up the sneakbox child's play. The brant limit in those years was three birds and as a rule one could bag a limit. Often, too quickly. Frosting on the cake out there on the bay edge of the strand were ducks of several species. Puddlers, mostly wigeon, but also pintail and teal. Now and then divers, bufflehead mostly, but on the rare occasion some bluebills and once in a while also cans. In my entire time on the Oregon coast I saw redheads only once. Four birds, all drakes, at Alsea, down the coast.

Back to the wigeon. It is still my favorite puddle duck. Believe me, many's the time that wigeon have, for me, made a duckless day one of victory in the last inning. An artist friend in England calls wigeon over there "Wogs". Nice ring to it—Wogs on the strand at Netarts as well as black brant ruled my roost and made up the bulk of my many bags there.

My friend, Worth Mathewson, writes in his recent book, *Big December Canvasbacks*, on the merit of the wigeon as a table bird. His conclusions are honest, I feel. This species can be excellent table fare and, then again, not so excellent. But for me, always worth bagging to eat whether it be a coastal bird or one from the Klamath Forest marsh. Off the strand, wigeon were almost always the "duck of the day", much to my delight.

Once the first afternoon's hunt was over, the decoys were drawn ashore and secured for the coming high tide. The sneakbox was also pulled up on the higher ground, and anchored fore and aft resting there on the salicornia grass. It was above the tide now, but later on before dark, we'd be afloat until the ebb in early morning.

Our supper was about as spartan as one could imagine—short of jerky and water. Lady fared well on her everyday ration of dry dog food and water. I ate a simple previously prepared ration. An example—a compressed egg sandwich and coffee made over a small backpacker's propane fuel stove. To make a compressed egg sandwich is a simple matter. In the predawn darkness, prior to departure for the coast, one fries one egg, breaking the yolk intentionally. Places the hot egg on a slice of "punk bread." This is the bread that sells for fifty cents per loaf, even now. This bread works best as it is so soft and wimpy. Sometimes referred to as "flaccid" by friends in the medical community. The addition of a little butter, mayonnaise, or whatever covered by a second slice of punk. One must work fast in assembling this sandwich for heat is one of the key elements for quality. Wrap hot sandwich in wax paper as tightly and neatly as possible. Place wrapped sandwich in small brown paper bag and seal. Place packet in a hip pocket at once. Sit on sandwich all the way over to coast. Sit on sandwich all day in sneakbox. When sandwich is unwrapped in late afternoon one is ravenous and by now the sandwich , although thinner, is twice the size as originally. Sitting on it for twelve hours has split the wrappings, allowing for this expansion. Surprisingly, the sandwich, if eaten immediately after unwrapping is still warm—just body temperature. I pass along this old family recipe as I'm a good guy at heart, and the recipe is truly time tested. A word of caution here. Do not be alarmed when you notice that the sandwich has an arc or curved appearance. The amount of curvature is determined by one's body contour.

A non-smoker by then, I didn't "sit over a pipe" and contemplate the waning day. Rather, we both settled in for the night, as the making tide made getting aboard the boat imperative. Lady bedded down under the after deck, her pallet a foam pad and dry burlap coffee sacks. I occupied the open cockpit area on a foam pad that doubled as a comfort pad when I hunted the box in layout mode. A lightweight down bag, my floatation jacket as a pillow comprised my "sack". On the Oregon coast in winter, the chance of rain was slightly less than inevitable, so some cockpit cover was mandatory. I used a plain old lightweight canvas tarp of ample size to cover the cockpit with plenty to spare. If heavy wind accompanied the wet stuff, it

took some doing to keep the tarp in place but for the most part we persevered. The fact that we made several of these hunts each season proves to me that the drill was not all that severe. Lady had no vote and voiced no complaints.

If I had figured my tides right, dawn found us hard aground on the salicornia grass flat. At once we could attend to morning "chores", take a limbering up walk over to the dunes and back and prepare breakfast. Again, Lady had her regular ration of dry food and a side of water. Usually a tidbit or so from my meal as well. My fare was also ultra simple. Coffee again made on the mountain stove. Over the first cup I'd whip up reconstituted eggs and fry. The eggs and ships crackers were always a favorite fare, likely because of the simplicity. After all, we were out here to hunt brant.

Food was way down low on the priority list. Once our bellies were satisfied, not taut, just satisfied, we set to rigging the decoys. They were simply pulled off the grass and into the water along the drop off. Very soon the making tide would float them level with the grass. The sneakbox was pulled once again over to the edge and minor repairs made to the grassing of the day before.

Often, on these early morning lows, bird action was slow. No problem, for here was the time to explore up and down the strand a little ways. Beach combing has long been a favorite pastime. I'd maybe shoot a snipe or two, or a scoter if they were trading over the strand into the bay. As we were never out of sight of our rig it was a simple matter to hustle back to the boat once the birds started to move.

Sometimes, not often though, the brant never did fly well. On these days, large flocks followed the tide in down bay, feeding on floating eelgrass as they floated along. I recall days when all of the brant I bagged were flushed from flocks as they fed on eelgrass while drifting past the blind. Not my

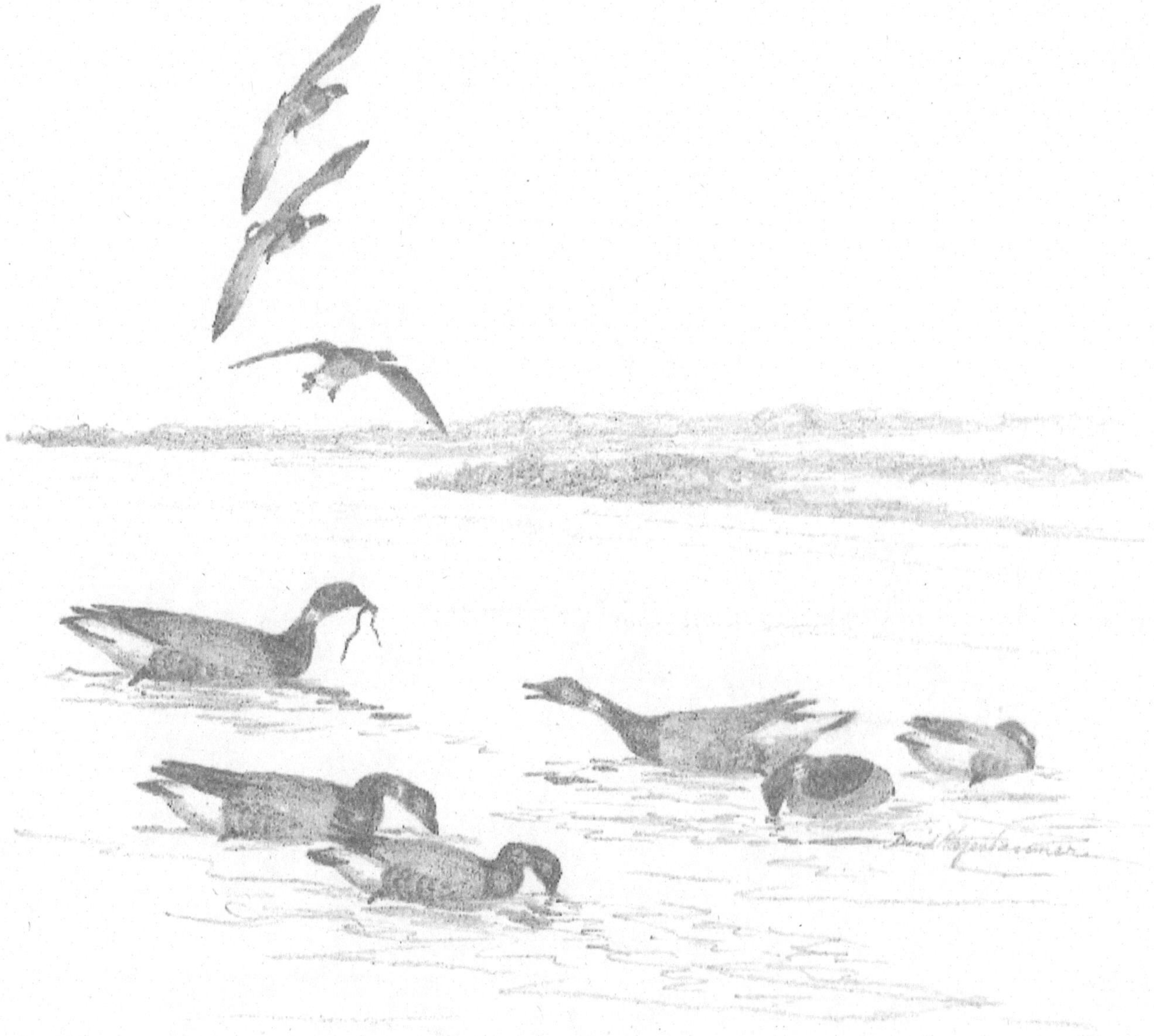

BRANT FEEDING ON FLOATING EELGRASS

favorite way to hunt brant but I always persevered. Such adversity I handle well.

On days of heavy weather, bird action was generally continuous. Both duck and brant. If our second day there was a bad weather day, and I foolishly launched up bay near town, some serious decision making was in order. Risk an up bay run, or dash across the short haul to the shelter of Whisky Crick, hitch hike a ride up to the launch in town, drive back to the Creek and load the sneakbox. Only a couple or so times I got myself in this fix. Guess I'm a slow learner. As I said earlier, these overnighters were only a now and then thing. Most of the time, to avoid the hassle of making that compressed egg sandwich I guess, Lady and I would pick a handy tide, drive to the bay, hunt three or four hours, and be back at the farm near dark.

At Netarts I had two other methods of hunting the bay. One, a launch in

CLARE EDNER - NETARTS, OREGON
SOLID RED CEDAR - 1938

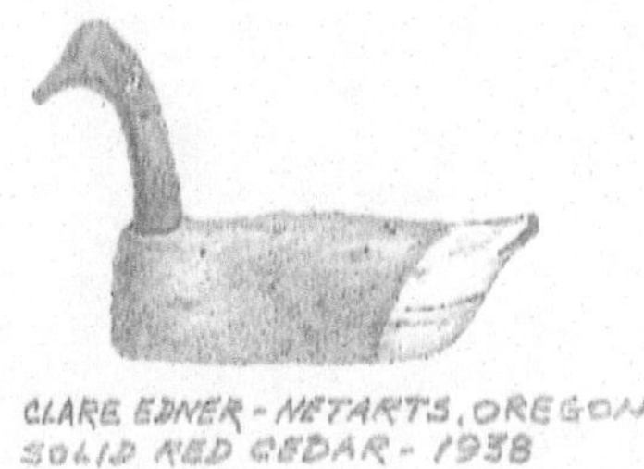

Whiskey Crick. A quick row out of the creek and only a couple of hundred yards into the bay proper. No Lady this time, just me and decoys for a layout hunt with as many brant decoys as I could get aboard the boat—about forty—set the rig in a fat line and anchor the boat parallel to the line of decoys. Shrimp net over the boat and some gull decoys on the decks and gunnels, my time proven layout for brant.

Another layout method was not on open water, but rather alongside a sand bar. Netarts had some channels throughout the entire bay. Some of these never went dry even on a low tide. Of course, winter daytime lows are never so severe as summer lows. Regardless, I would anchor the sneakbox along the edge of a sandbar that bordered one of these deeper channels. I'd use a couple of dozen shadows on the bar close by the boat and a couple of dozen floaters in the water close by the boat on the other side. Again shrimp net over the boat but I did not bother with the gull decoys on this hunt. Lady was with me on this hunt as she would lay on the sand among the shadows and retrieve from there. Hunting from the strand, after all is said and done, was my favorite method to gun for brant at Netarts.

In due course, I finally bumped into Wes Batterson. Over the years, Wes gained a reputation as the best brant caller on the coast and, of course, a brant hunter of renown. This first meeting was early one morning at the Netarts public boat launch in town. I was heading out to the upper end of the strand to hunt from the sneakbox alongside a huge grounded fir log. Wes was headed down bay by car to hunt with shadows from the shoreline at one of his favored spots. Our first meeting was brief due to pressing engagements on both of our parts. We'd meet again later on and get to know one another a tad better as we exchanged experiences. Wesley (Wes) M. Batterson was born in 1909 on the family homestead, near Nehalem, Oregon. In 1941 he was hired as a biologist by the Oregon State Game Commission; a position he held for thirty-four years.

In the early seventies I'd meet Wes from time to time at the boat launch at Netarts. We'd chat for a time, mostly about brant, but never got around to hunting together. Most likely because I hunted almost entirely by boat and Wes by that point in time would have nothing to do with boats. He had a close shave one time at Netarts involving a brant hunt, a boat, and a whopper of a storm. From that time on, Wes hunted brant only from the shorelines of Netarts and Tillamook; wadeable waters only. Several times as I drove along the bay road enroute to the Netart boat launch, I'd see Wes and a crony hunting brant on a sand bar within good view of the highway.

Those who knew this man well, rated him as the master brant voice caller of all time. I've long regretted that we didn't hunt together at least once so that I could have heard the virtuoso in action. Now and again during those years as I passed through the little town of Nehalem, I'd stop to see Wes, his aviary, and tell a brant story or two. We've lost touch, but I hear that Wes, at 87, still is active, steelheading and other outdoor related ventures. No writing or discussion regarding the North Pacific coast would ever be complete without the inclusion of Wes Batterson.

This section of the Oregon coast during the slot of 1964 - 1975 was the serious branter's utopia. Not only did this section of the coast still hold healthy wintering populations of brant but just as important the number of gunners seeking this species was small. It was a grand point in time for the branter. One day in particular stood out.

This was to be some brant and duck day. And a day to recall as one of the worst I'd experienced on Netarts with regard to winds. John Woodmark, a long time coastal resident crony, sneakbox user, and as avid a waterfowler as I, set up plans for a brant hunt on the bay. We wanted to rig a large spread of decoys, brant as well as ducks, since our plan was to hunt from our boats tied alongside an enormous fir log that had grounded and sanded in about a quarter mile from the public launch at Netarts. Even at low tide there was water around this log which protruded out at a slight angle, about thirty feet showing above the surface. This log still had some stubs of broken off limbs which made for easy tie up of the boats. I was to bring the Ducker and my sneakbox and John his Chesapeake, Luke, and his sneakbox with as

many decoys as he could manage. In total we'd have about six dozen decoys for our spread. It was more than needed, but it would please us.

We traveled in convoy over to the bay and upon arrival felt at once uneasy at the force of the wind. Since we'd be hunting in open water, this could be something to reckon with if the blow picked up. After a brief pow-wow, we both felt comfortable enough to go out as it was only a tad over fifteen hundred feet out to the log. We had good craft for such work, and knew small handling well. Before we launched I let the folks who ran the bar at the boat launch know we were going out and to where. Heck, you could see the log from the front window of the bar. On days with good visibility, that is.

During the night, a lot of eelgrass had floated into the boat launch and choked the concrete ramp to a depth of two feet. The removal of enough of this to get the boats in the water took a half hour or so and by now it was evident that the wind had grown a bit stronger. The Netarts public launch was very poorly engineered with respect to the direction it faces. Almost due south, the heaviest winter storms on the Oregon coast are southerly or southwesterly. As a result, this particular launch is fully exposed to the waves that march up bay ahead of these winds. No breakwater, no nothing—at least in the early seventies there was not.

John managed to get out of the launch by standing alongside his boat, starting the outboard and keeping the boat headed straight ahead and into the waves coming in. At the right moment, between waves he rolled into the cockpit, threw the engine into gear and took off. So far, so good. My turn now and it was a smidgen tougher. Towing the Ducker out of the launch was some doing. We'd discussed this earlier, and about just leaving the Ducker behind with the trucks. Since more than half of our decoy rig was in the Ducker, this didn't suit either of us. I was young then and figured I knew just how to pull this off. I stood in the water alongside my sneakbox, just as John had done. On the other side of the boat I had secured the Ducker so this way I was able to keep both boats headed right. In due course the right interval between waves came along. I piled into the cockpit, threw the Evinrude in gear and headed out. Once clear of the concrete sides of the ramp, I untied the after line of the Ducker so she could drop back and follow along behind under tow. John had laid off shore a hundred feet or so while I got underway. We regrouped and headed off in the direction of the log as best we could guesstimate the bearing. For by now, it had also started to rain. The log, a quarter of a mile out, was totally obscured.

After an interval of time had passed that I felt should have put us at the log there was no log yet. The situation had taken a change for the worse. If we couldn't find the log, how in blazes could we find the boat launch back there? This, however, was not that serious as by running downwind we would find the North Shore somewhere not too far from the launch. I took a sounding with an oar and we were by then in about three feet of water over a hard sand bottom. This was the bar where the log was—or had it moved since we'd last been there? All this time we had been making wide circles in an effort to locate that blamed log. All of a sudden there it was! On a circle upwind it loomed up just ahead.

I tied up the Ducker and we set to rigging the decoys we'd packed in our boxes. Once we'd done that the Ducker's decoys were divided and we worked together adding these to the spread. The visibility was so poor we elected to keep all of our decoys in view and this we figured amounted to barely fifty yards. During our decoy setting we saw no birds, brant or ducks. My personal view of the whole situation was one of total disgust. No birds would fly in this weather with near zero visibility. John was a bit more optimistic so we made a pact to stick it out for one hour. An ample time, we agreed, to see if anything would fly.

Time passed slowly as we worked at keeping our boats and the Ducker from being smashed against the log. The water at the log was by now only about knee deep as the tide was on the ebb—about low according to our watches and a tide book. I've long heard old timers claim that the winds change, either start or drop off in tune with tidal changes. How much of this is fact or fiction I'll never know, but as if on cue, the heavy winds started to moderate as the slack low tide time was near. In fact, the rain slacked off, then almost stopped so that directly we could make out the north shore launch area. Man, if only some birds would fly now. The set up was as perfect as one could dream of. The wind continued to slack off and in time was just a stiff breeze—perfect to keep decoying birds coming the way we intended as we set the decoys. The wind was at our backs, the decoys were behind and on both sides of us, birds decoying would be in our faces. Directly, gulls start-

EVART BOGE -
METAL SHADOW - 1938

EVART MADE LARGE RIGS OF BOTH
THESE DESIGNS - THEY WERE
USED ON NETARTS AND ON
TILLAMOOK BAYS

EVART BOGE - TILLAMOOK, ORE.
SOLID RED CEDAR - 1937

HUMBOLDT BAY, CA. — MOST LIKELY BILL PRINCHES

WES BATTERSON — NEHALEM, ORE.

BRANT DECOYING TO THE LOG RIG

ed moving about, and shore bird flocks passed by on their way closer in to the strand's beach not far behind our log. Soon, some ducks and a band of brant or two also came into view. Things were starting to shape up and now and then birds would decoy. In fact, Luke had his work cut out for him. We'd take a brant or so out of one bunch and before Luke could collect them, more would decoy. The limit was still three then and before our "pact" hour had passed we had six brant. A few ducks had decoyed but we agreed to hold off on them till we had our brant.

The rain still held off, but the wind seemed to be picking up. Nothing yet to fret over, so we held out hoping to get a few ducks. As if a spigot had been turned, ducks started to come out of the northwest right through the entrance of the bay and over us. It was very evident that these were migrating fowl. Some were quite high, most maybe, but now and again a bunch was lower and these looked us over. A bunch now and then actually decoyed. We shot ducks regularly, at least every ten or so minutes. Luke had no trouble keeping up with his chores. By now the wind was definitely building. It reached the point that we held a quick council and agreed to pack it in. The water was still only about knee deep, the bottom hard sand, so we waded beside our boats to speed up the pick up of our spread. Shortly,

all was in order. I had the Ducker in tow behind my sneakbox with the netting lashed over her load in case she rolled. Good move! As we moved toward the launch there was no doubt at all that the wind had once again built up to a force equal to that of the early morning. Maybe more.

Our plan was for John to go into the launch first and run up onto the foot or so of eelgrass still wind rowed there. This would protect his boat from damage on the concrete ramp. Once on the eelgrass he could pull his sneakbox further up and off to one side to give me room to follow on in. For me, with the Ducker in tow, it would be more complicated. The waves were piling straight into the launch and as the ramp was bordered by concrete walls it formed a sort of tunnel. The waves couldn't break and flatten, they just built up in there like sort of a devils cauldron.

During the time it took for John to get his boat in on the eelgrass and pulled up, I stayed a hundred or so yards out over deeper water where the waves were more regular and less choppy than inshore. On one of my circles out there the Ducker caught a beam sea and capsized! The net held the load of decoys in place and loaded to the gills, even under both decks she had 100% buoyancy. No danger of sinking, but upside down she towed poorly—"sorta" drunkenly. I couldn't risk trying to get her righted, just handling the sneakbox was a full time job. No conference now with John. He was on solid ground and I was out there.

John is a good man. He'd been watching me the whole time through glasses. He saw the Ducker roll, knew my dilemma , and also knew I'd have to figure it out for myself. If I had rolled the sneakbox as well he would have put his boat back in the water at once and been out to help me pronto. No need for that yet as I was still right side up. Have you ever taken notice of the way big waves "talk"? As they march by they give a sort of hissing sound. I sure heard plenty that day.

The course ahead for me and the Ducker was pretty straight forward. I had to take her in with me—but alongside, or towed? Upside down and partially filled with water, she towed like a dead cow. It was better to get her alongside and secure her fore and amid ships. My plan was to hold both lines in my right hand so I could run the outboard with my left. The drill was clear. I'd run into the launch tunnel as

John had done in hopes I could run the sneakbox up on the eel grass. At the last
moment I'd cast the Ducker's line free and concentrate on getting out of the
Barnegat as I cut the engine and bailed out. I knew full well that John would be
there in water up to his waist waiting to corral the Ducker as I cast her free. I knew
that he knew exactly what I had planned. I laid off the launch briefly hoping to get
a break between waves, but those following seas were murder as I lost steerageway.
The hell with it, I gave the Evinrude throttle and bore ahead for that eelgrass cushion. John was right there as I knew he'd be—up to his waist and ready. I cast the
Ducker loose and almost at once was on the eelgrass. I chopped the power, bailed
out, got the bow line and pulled the sneakbox on up as high as I could muscle her.
Not until then could I look to see how John and the Ducker fared. There he stood,
alongside the Ducker—up high and dry! I should'a known. It was, I guess, the first
time I really had a chance to be scared. Too much going on all at once to dwell on
it before now. Once we had our boats on their trailers and the Ducker in my pickup did we really slack off and start to appreciate having a saloon so close at hand!

While Netarts held most of my attention close by, the larger Tillamook, in due
course, had to be hunted. This bay is the third largest of Oregon estuaries with a
whopping eight-thousand acres! Several rivers run into Tillamook, and so create
huge marshy deltas where duck hunting can be exceptional for those who study
tides and their effects on duck movements. For the branter at Tillamook the best
bet in my time there, was a minuscule sandbar in the SW corner of the bay and all

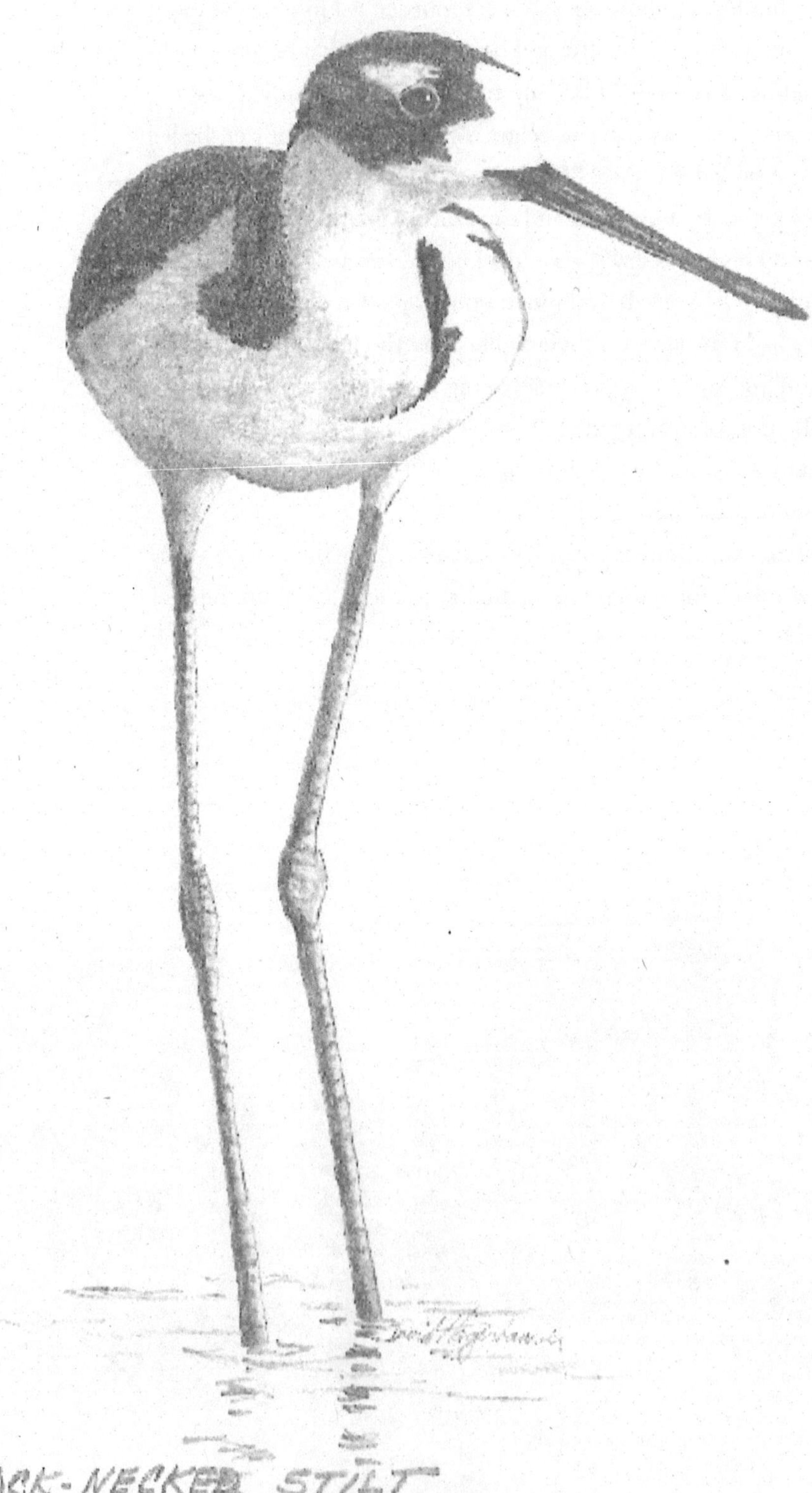

BLACK-NECKED STILT

along the Bay Ocean Spit. Yet another option was to use a layout rig in the open water of the SW corner of the bay. This area served me best.

Circa 1915, a group of Portland, Oregon investors started a development on the strand that separates Tillamook bay from the Pacific Ocean. Roads were built, a huge hotel that boasted a pool and arboretum was constructed, a post office and stores soon followed. Lots were offered for sale and advertised on a nationwide scale. As homes were built, the developers started an excursion train from Portland that took potential lot buyers to Tillamook and then embarked them on a boat over to Bayocean. Few stones were left unturned in efforts to attract new citizens.

By the thirties, over one-hundred homes had been built. Although the depression slowed building somewhat, it did continue into the forties. About this time, a redesign of one of the entrance jetties of Tillamook bay caused a change in ocean currents that started serious erosion of the strand at Bayocean. Several homes actually fell into the sea because of this. A whopper of a storm finished what the currents had started and the strand was breached. Citizens of Bayocean began to abandon the town. A few toughed it out and stayed on until the fifties when another huge storm wiped out most of what remained.

Scotch broom and other hardy beach growth quickly started to heal the scars and shortly little was left to show that Bayocean ever existed. Natural events also healed the storm caused breach in the strand. I understand that still today one can, by diligent search, find traces of the town in the scotch broom thickets. Water pipes, slabs of asphalt roadway, railroad track, and other odds and ends of civilization; momentos of man's intrusion into a habitat where he did not belong.

Tucked away, and unknown to some, was a tiny sandbar in Tillamook's extreme southwestern corner. It lay but a short distance off the main shore of the bay. Perhaps on a daylight winter tide it was two-hundred feet long. After an absence of almost a quarter century I could be off a tad. As the tide ebbed to a certain level the bar appeared. In short order one should be on it if one had plans to set shadows and hunt. For this sand bar the Ducker was the ticket. There is no boat launch here so all craft launched had to be man handled. Today, such a situation is marked on maps as "unimproved"! I'd load the Ducker with a couple of dozen shadows and push off for the bar only a few paddle strokes off. Sometimes, I set out even before the bar showed if time for whatever reason was of the essence. Once at the bar I set the shadows and some flags among them. The Ducker was pulled ashore at a far end of the bar and covered with net. I crouched or laid in the shadows wearing a black raincoat. This was just about as simple as a decoy hunt could be made. Sometimes it worked if the brant were using that end of the bay, a limit came easily. Some days all that stirred over the bar were the ever present gulls. So soon I came to the conclusion that this bar hunt was also a "crap shoot." The bar did not lure back often but so long as I lived in Independence I went back now and again. It was, after all, sorta unique.

Now and again when I needed a Tillamook "fix" I'd walk down the Bay Ocean Spit with a pack frame loaded with shadows, flags and an entrenching tool, "MK. IV!" Lady always accompanied me on the spit trips as her duty out there was indis-

SOFT-SHELL CLAM

pensable. Besides all that, it was a lark even if no birds were brought to bag, which was usually the case. Overall, my trips to Tillamook were infrequent when compared to those I made at Netarts just over the hill. My memories of that big bay will always be special. If for no other reason than it's size. The waters appeared vast when compared to tiny Netarts. The force of it's storms seemed to be in proportion to the size of the bay. To me, everything about Tillamook seemed enormous. In it's own way, Tillamook deserves, and has, a special niche in my roster of brant bays.

On the north shore of Tillamook lies the town of Garibaldi. Here also is the delta of the small Miami River. Maps give it the honorary name of river. I'd rate it more of a big "crick". Anyhow, on the southern border of the Miami's delta were very productive cockle clam beds. These hard shell clams live very close to the mud/sand surface, are easily raked up, and are strong in flavor. In my estimation, they make the best clam chowder of any of the Oregon coast bivalves. A good share of my Tillamook adventures would include a brief stop at the Miami river for some "chowder clams".

To depart Tillamook with no mention of the duck hunting there would be unfair. In my time, this area was lightly hunted and with a sneakbox I found easy access into this marsh and its labyrinth of tidal guts and dreens. Here, on a making tide, puddle ducks flooded into the marsh in numbers to boggle the mind. Again wigeon were the predominate species, and again I say whoopee! Never once on Tillamook did I make any effort to target the divers. On hunts there, some were seen but as I recall, never in numbers that would tempt a fellow to rig the big spread necessary.

GULLS AT REST AND A WING

A ways down coast is Yaquina Bay. Alongside sits the town of Newport. Here in the decade of '64 to '75 this estuary still supported a decent brant wintering population. I'd guess maybe five-hundred or more birds. Most used in an area named Sally's Bend on the bay's northern shore—only slightly up bay from town. The birds did, of course, move about and to hunt them a couple of other locations were worthwhile.

Young Vic Coggins, whom I met in Ashland a few years before, was now attending Oregon State University in Corvallis. Vic, as well as a Joe Chapman, also at OSU, fell in with me during my tenure in the Independence area, and we made many waterfowl hunts together.

One winter during brant season, Vic and I set up a hunt on Yaquina Bay. The town of Newport lies on the north shore of this three thousand acre highly commercial bay. Our plan was to launch my Gregor skiff at the town's public sling launch and then cross the bay and hunt the sand bar at the mouth of Kings Slough. Once on the bar we would rig fifty shadows and simply lean over in sit-down pits among the spread wearing rain gear. This was an ultra simple method of mine for gunning brant on the sandbars of all the Pacific estuaries. Uncomplicated, yet effective. We would simply pull our skiff ashore a couple of hundred yards down the bar. On a commercial bay such as Newport, boats and ships of all sizes were

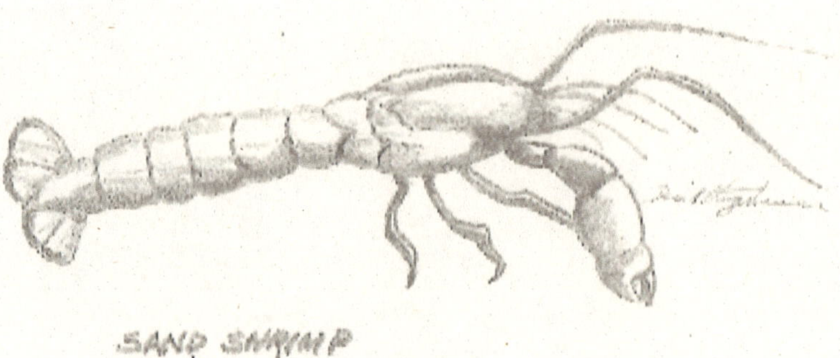

commonplace and brant paid them little heed.

Driving across the Coast Range in the pre-dawn darkness the truck's radio came forth with an unsettling weather report. The Coast Guard was predicting high winds for the entire Oregon Coast. Winds that could reach gusts of ninety plus MPH by noon. Not the weather I'd have chosen, but since the plan was to gun from a sand bar accessible by land there was no cause for panic. As we neared the coast the winds force was at once very apparent. But still no reason for concern. Once in Newport at the launch and with day breaking I saw at once the folly of crossing the "lumpy" bay to reach the bar. We simply drove through town and crossed the bay over the Hwy 101 bridge. This bridge slung high over the bay was swaying in the wind to such an extent the movement could be felt as we drove

across. Once over on the south side of the bay we parked in the OSU's Science Center. We left the skiff trailered and packed our shadows, guns, shovel, etc. up the bay shore a quarter of a mile or so to the site at King's Slough that we wanted to rig out. The light, what there was of it, was full by now, and the wind a force to reckon with. Few birds were flying—an oddball gull or two. Little rain was coming down but as we set the shadows it was evident that the wind was mounting. Once we'd set the silhouettes, with a good deal of difficulty, there seemed little reason to bother with the digging of sit down pits, as by now no birds of any kind flew. The shore-birds of several species simply huddled in groups all about us on the bar—every bill pointed directly into the gale. The bay was a cauldron of huge white horses, the spume so dense that the town of Newport only a half mile across the bay was obscured. Vic and I huddled on our knees among the shadows with butts facing the wind. To look into it was to be stung by a thousand bees— in this case grains of sand traveling at ninety plus miles per hour.

Our rain gear was plastered by wet sand and felt like body armor to move about. One by one the shadows, held in the sand by sturdy aluminum angle stakes were bent over till the decoy was almost parallel to the sand bar. After less than an hour, that seemed like several, we made an easy decision to pack it in. Walking out from the parking area, the westerly pushed us along but the return was another matter for sure. Burdened by the strings of shadows, and other gear, the quarter mile back was a trek I'll never forget. Likely, Vic will not either. Once in the truck and out of the wind my face felt like it was thawing out after a minor frost bite. Never before nor since have I been out in winds of such force. Winds that the Coast Guard reported later in the day to have gusted at plus 100 miles per hour at the Yaquina Bay entrance.

Once back across the bridge, our traditional stop at "MO's" on the waterfront for "Slumgullion" was as always one of any day's highlights. This day, especially so. Uncle Ed's phrase? "The wind blew, the crap flew, and I couldn't see for an hour or two." I should substitute sand for the wind borne material. Like every day afield, or amarsh there is always something to prompt recall. The storm day at Yaquina, circa 1971 was a classic!

I discovered "Mo's" and "slumgullion"—(a bowl of clam chowder with bay shrimp added) soon after I'd settled in Independence. A stop at Mo's soon became routine whether I was over at Yaquina Bay for waterfowling, crabbing, floundering or just passing through. Mo Niemi started her chowder house in 1951 on the waterfront in Newport, Oregon. The building had been an eatery since 1912, but once Mo reopened, it became a chowder house. Very soon after opening as Mo's a car slammed into the front of the building breaking most of the windows. Rather than rebuild the framework and replace the windows, Mo had a large overhead garage door installed. It remains so today. Perhaps it is opened on warm summer days to enliven the somewhat dark interior. I personally have never seen it opened and I've "chowdered down" at Mo's countless times.

As fame of her chowder grew, Mo gradually opened several other restaurants on the Oregon coast. Also an annex across the street from the original Mo's. One day after a duck/brant hunt, Vic and I stopped in Mo's for a traditional bowl and a sandwich. For whatever reason I didn't get the sandwich I'd ordered. When I meekly complained, the amazon of a waitress looming above me snarled "at Mo's you order what you want, but you eat what you get"! I did! The unexpected at Mo's only makes it the more colorful, although her famous chowder is reason enough for a stop on the Newport waterfront, if you should be passing through this little town on the coast Hwy101.

Yaquina Bay, for me, provided a good deal more days on the water for other critters than for fowl. Here on Yaquina I did my first "freelance crabbing." One day, I rented crab rings, bought bait, and set out in my own skiff to learn the drill. It was an experience I can tell you! The pull of that first ring was almost scary. It was full of crabs, mostly small ones, but crabs, at least. They spilled into the skiff's bottom and once scurried about like little demons intent on bodily harm. In short order I got the handle on things and soon caught a few "keepers". My destiny as a crabber was sealed. I pursue the tasty "beasties" still.

Now and again I did hunt ducks on Yaquina almost always on Kings Slough on the southern side of the bay directly across from the town. Rather narrow, I thought then to warrant a name so noble as KING . I hunted it for wigeon mostly, and sometimes it was very good, especially on stormy days when a lot of ducks sought shelter in the slough. In truth, I mention Kings Slough only as a place I hunted on Yaquina Bay.

On the south shore of Yaquina were many acres of clam beds. On a low summer tide, these vast beds were exposed for the digging of several species of clams. Gapers, and cockles mostly. The Gaper or "horse clam" is a large bi-valve that lives rather deep in the mud. Generally, about a couple of feet below the surface. To dig one out, one had to be prepared to expend some real effort. The quarry, if caught, is very impressive. Perhaps a pound or more of clam! Very tasty when prepared in several ways. Cockles live close to the surface and are mainly used minced for chowder. The meat is very tough, but flavorful, so use in chowder has evolved as the best way to use them.

On high tide and above these same clam beds on the South side of the bay were prime floundering grounds. As the tide made, the flounder fishermen anchored their boats here. The tide rose and the starry flounder followed it in over these mud flats in search of food. Favorite baits were clam necks or sand shrimp. Undoubtedly both baits aroused flounder's interest because both baits lived on these same flats. With crab, clams and fish available during the pleasant summer time, I spent more time on Yaquina Bay in summer than for waterfowl in winter.

Down coast a bit from Yaquina, lays Alsea Bay. It is a small estuary of only nine hundred acres. It was about as pristine then as a coastal bay could be. About all that occurred on these bay waters was some bait digging by hand—nothing commercial, but one old codger who couldn't throw in his towel still rig netted for crab on a commercial license. There were no brant on Alsea Bay but there was good duck

BASKET COCKLE CLAM

BAND-TAILED PIGEON - INSULATION CORK
BODY- PENCIL BILL - PAINTED EYES -
CLOTHESPIN FOR LIMB ATTACHMENT -
BY JAY LONG - CORVALLIS, OREGON -
CIRCA 1935 ·

hunting. I'll take that back about the brant. I did see one once. It was an immature bird, early on in the duck season. This poor confused youngster was standing on the breakwater one morning as I launched at McKinley's Marina to go out duck hunting. Later, I was told that the dock owner's son had shot the brant from the dock.

Alsea was the only estuary that I counted on for quality canvasback gunning. Back then, the bay supported a wintering population of some three or four-hundred cans that fed primarily on a fingernail clam. One would think that a main diet of clams of any sort would impart strange flavor to a duck, but not so in this case—those cans were as savory as any I've ever eaten. But then, a friend once said to me, "Dave, you're an eater, not a taster."

For cans at Alsea, I worked one spot, hunt after hunt. It was on the east side of the bay and here a small grass covered island stood out a bit from the rest of the marsh. An arm of the Alsea river formed a channel in front of the island. For reasons still unknown to me, there was a daily canvasback flight upstream and past the island. This flight coincided with a rising tide.

I hunted Alsea mostly with one of my sneakboxes and simply tied it up alongside the sheer bank of this little island that I soon gave the name "Barnegat Island". Backed by the island, little grassing of the boat was necessary. Often, I did none at all. I would rig about thirty can decoys, sometimes a few wigeon as well. It was a rare day indeed that one drew a blank on cans at Barnegat Island. The limit then was two as I recall, so wigeon could also be counted on for some action.

Wood ducks are not known for their abundance on Oregon's estuaries. In fact, in all the years I gunned this coast I encountered wood ducks only once on the salting. This was on an early morning of a season's opening. A nice bundle of mid-sized ducks decoyed, and my partner and I took five right off. To my surprise, as I picked them up all were young woodies. The light was not good that early, and in silhouette I simply took them for wigeon. What a surprise!

There was a productive soft shell clam bed alongside the island and often I dug clams before or after my hunt—or during a lull. Way down bay nearer the ocean, crabbing was also a favored activity for many of us who frequented this bay.

State Highway 34 over to Waldport on Alsea Bay goes through some of the Coast Range's finest band-tailed pigeon habitat; as did Highway 20 over to Yaquina Bay. Names of some of those small towns stir my memory still. How about Tidewater, Wren, Blodgett, Burnt Woods and Eddyville? All bring back visions of the past when I pursued those gray ghosts of the misty coast range hillsides. Side hills were cloaked with elderberry brush and at times alive with wild pigeons. Worth Mathewson, who lives in that area still, tells me that pigeon hunting in Oregon is just about a thing of the past. There remains a two bird limit in a season of a week or less.

This sounds very much like our brant hunting here in Washington which has a ten day season and a two bird limit. This has been in effect for several years. It has not fazed me to see this restriction. I still savor the bird or two I take each season. Perhaps, it makes my hunts more special. I have friends who go on a sage grouse hunt each season. Sage grouse also have very limited seasons. I sense that these rigid restrictions make their bird or two every year a trophy. On the other hand, one could take the stand that if a species is in any sort of jeopardy—number-wise, habitat loss, whatever—then there should be NO season at all. I don't know the correct course. Game managers have, for years, been doing it both ways.

Once in Independence I fell in with the Oregon State University "crowd". This would be, specifically, a bunch of the guys in the wildlife and fisheries part of the school. And, to be more specific, those guys that actually hunted and fished. Like Vic Coggins, Joe Chapman and Jay Long.

Jay was the kingpin of this group. At the time of our meeting, he was a professor at the school and taught wildlife subjects; had been doing so for almost thirty years by then and was some fifty years old when our paths crossed. Jay was a very soft spoken man, had a wealth of friends, and so far as I'm concerned, knew more about how to hunt and fish the state of Oregon than anyone I'd ever met.

Oregon used a segment of its State police force in the enforcement of hunting and fishing laws. After regular police academy training these recruits attended Jay's wildlife courses at Oregon State University before assuming their duties as "game cops". I mention this about Jay so you'll understand that he was a very well known man in the wildlife circles of the State. Through the years Jay and I hunted and fished together a lot; hunted mostly. Knowing "everybody who was anybody" in the game world, Jay belonged to many clubs as an honorary member, and to others because he actually designed the hunt club and was given a membership in payment for services. As a friend of Jay's, I was treated to hunts at goose, duck, and pigeon clubs on a regular basis. Mostly though, Jay and I hunted together as freelancers since this was my favorite M.O.

I was the one who had the decoys, boats, and other gear necessary for serious waterfowling. It was gear that Jay did not have as it was unnecessary for the club hunter. It followed then, that for the most part our hunts together were in pursuit of ducks on either the Willamette River or on Alsea Bay.

From my diary: January 6, 1971, Barnegat Island.

Jay, Bob, Dave - 0810 - 1300 - Heavy rain - So Wind - 15 all day.

This was really some day! Jay really had a good time, as did we.

Eighteen birds - 16 bull cans, 1 G. scaup drake, one Surf Scoter drake.

I include this diary entry with some embellishment. Jay was a shooter of double guns and prided himself on his shooting ability with the scattergun; rightly so, as he was an exceptional shot. Anyhow, we had bagged the sixteen canvasbacks and the bluebill and were set to pickup when along came this big old drake surf scoter. He wasn't decoying, just passing by out beyond the decoys. Jay was shooting one of his monster three inch twelves that day—loaded with copper plated threes, his favorite "big duck" loads; hand loaded to his specs. Anyhow, I allowed as to the bird being way outa' range when Jay ups and dumps that "skunkhead" stone cold! As best as I could guesstimate, at least sixty yards; more likely closer to seventy. I took the bird home for "coot stew".

During the duck and goose season, Jay wore his badge of honor. This being a heavily taped finger on his right hand as protection against the abuse of his double gun's trigger guard. Those three inch "Roman Candles" were potent! Jay used a lot of Tums. I have no idea for certain why. However it was likely because of his favorite combo of chili peppers and vodka. Anyway, one time on a grouse hunt he was reloading and unknowingly dropped a roll of Tums into his gun barrel. As the antacids dropped through the gun's tube and at his feet, those present had fodder for a lot of ribbing in "fat chewing sessions" to come. Jay took such things in stride.

Jay Long was the gent who tagged me with the label of being an eater and not a taster. The man was a fine cook. Especially when he cooked wild game. My wife, Delphie, and I visited Jay in Yuma, Arizona five or six years ago and he insisted on preparing a lunch of shrimp and other goodies. His old cat, George, sat on one edge of the table overseeing the entire meal. We never saw our dear friend after that day. He died in 1995.

This chapter would be desperately incomplete without a story or so that included my good cronies, Joe Chapman and Vic Coggins. Very soon after arriving in Corvallis our paths crossed. Joe, at OSU, was working on post graduate projects—papers on field research, monographs on several species, you name it, Joe had studied it—from dusky Canada geese to cottontails.

I'd known Vic since Ashland days. He lived with his family and attended High School there before going to Oregon State University in Corvallis. I had kept tabs on Vic and knew he was at OSU. Once we'd met and confirmed the fact that the three of us were afflicted with the same disease—waterfowling—the die was cast. Joe, Vic and I became almost inseparable as duck hunters in the Independence era. Strangely though, Joe and I hunted together only on the Willamette for ducks and geese. Only a time or two did he accompany me to the coast for ducks—not at all for brant, that I recall.

Joe had a great hulk of a yellow Lab. "Cougar", by name—Lambie Pie in disposition. Joe had got "Coug" as a pup, trained him himself to a point that they started entering local field trials. Cougar was a natural, and soon the trials were on the State level. Joe speaks with pride of that day when Cougar had just won first in a State event and a fellow offered him $10,000 for "your dog". Joe's pride stems from the fact he did not have to deliberate in saying "no". " Not no, but hell no!" Now and again, to this day, I think of Joe's dilemma at that moment in time. A student, scratching for funds as many must do, and ten big ones waved in your face! Some decision to make, eh?

All of us were decoy hunters—still are. Between us we had plenty of decoys. Some Herter's plastics and some worn down Custon-Bilts. We splurged and added three or so dozen more Herter' model 72 mallards to our rig, also some Otter geese. These I quickly repainted and we were in business.

Joe had been using an able boat for his river hunting before we met. While able for his needs it was far too small for two hunters and a lot of decoys. And, I mean a lot! In shopping around the local marinas a decent sixteen footer turned up and I

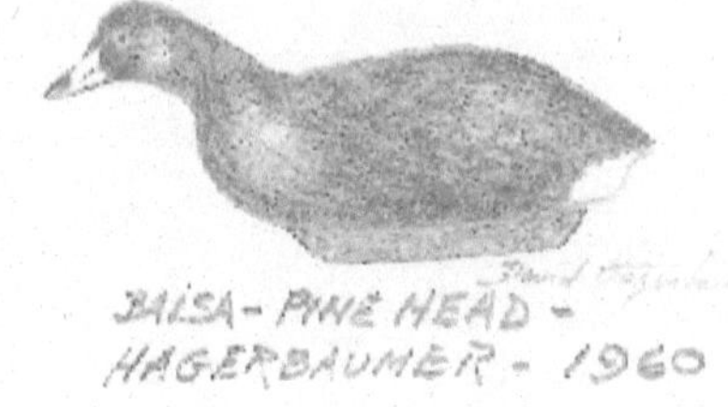

bought it, also a new Evinrude. We had plenty of boat then and really went at it.

The Willamette River, as you likely know, flows north and into the Columbia at Portland. The Willamette around the stretch we used was a medium sized stream much in character like my beloved Mississippi—cottonwoods, willows, sand and gravel bars, and a wealth of sloughs and oxbows. Never once did I set up on the Willamette to hunt ducks that I did not reminisce a bit.

Joe, Vic and I hunted, for the most part, that stretch of the river from Albany upstream to about Halsey—about a thirty mile stretch as the mallard flies. Perhaps thirty-five as the river flowed. This stretch held a wealth of sloughs and gravel bars and we soon homed in on several as the best suited for our style of decoy hunting. Right off the bat some names come to mind all of these thirty-five years later. Names the two of us gave these spots for whatever reasons. "Panic Slough", because of a hectic hunt we had there once which I'll explain in a short story further on. "Howards Place", that Joe named in memory of one of his teachers who died at far too early an age. "Mink Bar", because I once saw a mink there as I sat in my blind. "Cougar Slough", after the finest retriever I've ever hunted with. "The Island", that also deserves more than mention. These are but a few of those that we hunted regularly.

While Joe had a deep love for Coug, there were those times when both Vic and I had our doubts. There must have been a time of perfection early on when Cougar and Joe won many honors around Oregon in the trials. As the years passed, however, both of them grew a tad

lax and the big dog back-slid a little. Little things would happen. Cougar would break as the shooting started and be out there in the water among the decoys waiting for ducks to fall—even before they died—sorta like a player in centerfield. I secretly felt it very entertaining, but dared not share my mirth as Joe took it all as a personal affront. That his dog would pull such shenanigans, a field trial dog at that, was not to be tolerated. In spite of the fact that Joe himself let Coug's training sorta slide as the years wore on. Anyhow, the "punishment" was always the same after one of these entertaining infractions. Cougar would swim back to the boat with duck in mouth amid the wild shouting of his master. Usually Coug would manage (on these occasions) to become entangled in the net blind of the boat and or drag several decoys along as he swam back. This, of course, fueled Joe's fire. Once aboard, Joe would take Cougar's snout in his hand and tell him just how the "cow ate the cabbage" as he screamed at the dog—their noses pressed together. Cougar never even took a deep breath over these tirades, but Joe would turn purple. Even at his young age, I was fearful he'd have a coronary. And so it went for several delightful seasons.

Perhaps one out of three hunts included a guest. Mostly Joe's friends at Oregon State. When a guest came along Joe used his old boat for he and Coug and I took the extra guy with me. Chuck Henny was a frequent guest. Chuck enjoyed duck hunting but not enough to have the necessary equipment. He and Joe were working together on their monograph under the direction of their teacher, Howard Wight, who passed on a bit later. On this particular morning, the three of us, Cougar, Joe and I pulled into a slough we really favored. We almost always had good luck there. My diary records the day as December 8, 1967. We rigged our boat alongside a small island that lay at the slough's eastern end. This was a large slough, at least two hundred yards long by one hundred wide. A narrow gravel bar covered with short willows separated the slough from the river. At the end where the island was located, the slough opened into the river. When the river was high, only the willows on the narrow bar showed their tops and the slough seemed almost part of the river—current and all. On this day we chose to hunt from the island as the river was high and only the island provided the high ground we liked to blind up against. Noted also in my diary—

"Wind - easterly, Temperature - 45-50 degrees, rain squalls. Set up
at 1300 - some birds all afternoon, but high. Saw many all at once—
about 1615 - tried to land in upper end of slough. Panic took over
at this point." We bagged three mallards and one green-winged teal.

My diary does not note that when we gave the slough the name of "Panic" that day, the real reason was not the sudden influx of ducks that refused to decoy only to land in the far end of the slough but rather our poor marksmanship, several occasions when we shot the same birds from decoying flocks, the loss of a cripple (rare), and in general an overall poor performance by two experienced waterfowlers and one field trial retriever. The sudden appearance of a couple of hundred mallards and wigeon that refused to decoy, was only the straw that broke our backs and pushed us over the edge.

Tagging this slough with the name "Panic" was a natural reflex. A season or two later, Joe and Chuck were to find a body hung up on a snag near the little island. This on an early and foggy morning as they pulled in to Panic to set up. After this incident I was unable to get Joe to hunt with me there for a couple of weeks. I can't really fault him as I found a body on the Willamette as well sometime

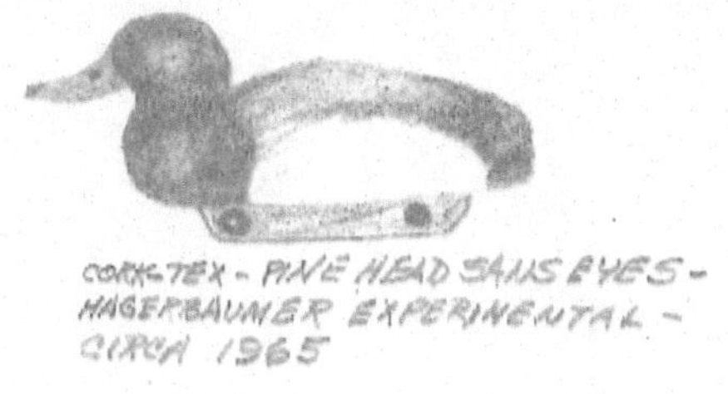

CORK-TEX - PINE HEAD SANS EYES - HAGERBAUMER EXPERIMENTAL - CIRCA 1965

before. I still remember the shock of seeing the moss covered and bloated form floating near some brush where I often jigged for crappie. It took some clenching of my teeth to get around to tying the body to the brush so it would be there when I later led a couple of the sheriff's deputies back to the spot.

And so the seasons went. My diary shows the Willamette hunting as starting in 1965 and the last season covered as 1971. I believe this to be correct, but my diary keeping has always been sporadic, so it could well be that a year or two have been omitted on one end or the other, or both.

Again from the diary: "November 11, 1966. Vic (Coggins) and Dave - Slough at Island - Set up at 0730 - Temp. 40 degrees - Rain moderate to heavy - Wind light to moderate out of South - Six mallard drakes - Four mallard hens. Saw lots of birds right away - limits by 0830. Hunted from boat with net and top up. Birds decoyed perfectly. Some landed close by boat. None saw us at any time while decoying."

The foregoing is the somewhat terse, though accurate, diary account. What the entry lacks, is the following that I recall vividly.

Vic and I pulled into the Slough at Island early in the morning. This slough was a couple of miles above the Albany launch. Once we had the boat tied up and netted over, I instructed Vic to stay aboard, load up, and I'd set the decoys. At this spot we seldom used more than eighteen or twenty oversize mallards so to rig this few took only twenty or so minutes. I'd no sooner started when Vic shot a mallard. I hustled to get the decoys rigged and the mallards kept coming. Vic would alert me to approaching birds and I'd crouch over in the decoys stock still. Soon Vic had his limit down. I was not done with the decoys so told Vic to take them as they came. By the time the decoys were out there were ten mallards on board. I'd done the retrieving as well as setting the decoys which now I started picking up again. This time with Vic's help. Never before or since have I gone through this exact drill. Quite an experience!

Both Joe and I are fair to middling duck callers. He used only a green hard plastic call named the KUM-DUK, made somewhere in Oregon, as I recall. It took a ton of air to activate this call and Joe was the dude who could do it. After all the exercise his lungs had from yelling at Coug, blowing that call was a breeze. As he called he also grunted on the inhale, and should a flock take a lot of "working" Joe would often turn purple from the over exertion. Again, I'd stew over his well being! At that time, I was favoring the Faulk line of calls. Easy to blow, great sound, and designed so one could retain his normal facial hue while calling through extended sessions.

We both shot twelve gauge guns. Joe, a Model 12 Winchester, and me, a Browning Auto Five, or my 1929 Model 11 Remington. Joe loved his Model 12 as he did Coug—completely. One day his barrel blew off. Joe reloaded and once in awhile he'd have a blooper. You know the kind. A poof, and the shot barely rolls out of the end of the barrel. We'll never know what the exact cause was, but from the outset I suspected that a wad got lodged at the choke. In any event, Joe was not injured when about four inches of the end of the barrel was opened up—the metal simply curled back in strips like an old blunderbuss. When Joe had stopped sobbing I reminded him of how the barrel resembled a blunderbuss or maybe even the end of a French horn. I was only trying to insert a bit of levity into this wake, but damned if he didn't start to blubber all over again.

In due course, Joe took the only way out and had a Poly-Choke installed. The only way out if he wanted to continue using that particular barrel. After he started using the gun again with the Poly hanging out there on the end I made the mistake one day of saying that his Model 12 looked pregnant and "was he planning to raise Winchesters?" Blamed if he didn't choke up all over again. While his Model 12 was at the gunsmith's I loaned him my Model 11, but only after he posted bond!

Another time both my guns were laid up and Joe's had a broken ejector or such. Desperate times demand desperate remedies so I loaned Joe an old bolt action Mossberg 12 gauge I had and I resorted to the sweet little Fox 410 double that Louie had given me years before. Sometime later I gave the Mossberg to Vic for a "survival" gun. With some trepidation, so armed, we hunted the first time on Cougar Slough. The "four ten" was chambered for three inch shells so I felt confident that with number six shot and a range of twenty-five yards or less I could do well. Joe, of course, could use 12 gauge duck loads so he was in good shape other than having to operate that bolt! The first go round went really well. I stuck to my plan and shot only birds at ranges of less than thirty yards. So far as results for me went I saw no difference in my effectiveness than with my twelve bores. With Joe, it was only a matter of fighting that clumsy bolt for a second shot. Otherwise, Joe did his usual good shooting. Joe was one of those "natural" shot gunners. His reflexes were sharp, he could estimate ranges, knew his species, and all in all was a disgustingly fine and consistent scatter gun man.

One event of the Cougar Slough hunt stands out in my recall. A lone dusky Canada goose flew up along the far side of the slough. As it came abreast, and at the closest point it would get, I let off a round from the 410. Blamed if that goose didn't come down! Appeared stoned, but it was only a crip that Coug retrieved easily. We both agreed that it was a forty yard shot. Ballistic experts say that the gauge does not determine the range, only the amount of shot delivered to that point. True, perhaps, but I'll never feel comfortable using a four ten on ducks or geese. Very soon, our guns were repaired, and we were using "duck guns" once more. But that brief interval with the Mossberg and the Fox was an interesting change.

For a lot of years I've steered away from body counting. Once I outgrew the "limit out" syndrome, the numbers game didn't sit too well with my newly acquired "purity". Anyhow, right here I am going to give a few figures. For example, in the 1968-69 season, Joe, Vic and I took three hundred and sixty ducks in forty-four hunts. This total includes those taken by the occasional guest.

In the season of 1970-71, the limit on canvasback in the Pacific Flyway was relaxed and made the same as for mallards or teal, for example. In this case, six birds per day. With an unheard of bonanza at hand I spent many days on the coast at Alsea Bay. Here there were canvasbacks, I knew how to hunt this bay, and now was a time that I felt would never come again. Between the river, Alsea Bay and some odd hunts over Klamath way, our guests and we three took four-hundred and thirty-three ducks. One hundred and one of this total were cans—only one hen.

There, I've done it! I feel these brief figures will help to illustrate the quality of the waterfowling in Oregon during my years there. It was not a sure thing, however, just to be on the Willamette River and to throw out a spread of decoys. My diary:

> "1966-Nov. 5-Joe and Dave - Three Bling Slough - At tip of
> Kiger Island. Set up at 3 p.m. - Temp. 40-45 degrees - wind light
> out of south -overcast with rain squalls. Both Island and Turaduck
> Point had other spreads so we used the slough below. Set out only
> three feeder strings plus eight or ten coot and wigeon. Saw a lot
> of birds high south, also several flocks of geese going south. Had two
> mallards work us several swings but they would not come in.
> It was a bust! It took Cougar to keep us from being "skunked"!

This refers to a crippled hen mallard the dog found in the brush behind our blind.

Waterfowling is seldom, if ever, a sure thing anyplace I know of. As great as the Willamette River was then, it was no exception to this rule. All good things must end, I guess, and the "little Mississippi" and the great waterfowling it offered started to go down hill fast. Time was marching on, and as it did so did the valley start to change. For most folks I suppose the changes were for the better. Not so for me, loner of old.

Smokeless industries, although small, started to crop up like morels on a moist and warm May morning. The three local refuges very quickly drew most of the wintering waterfowl to their thousands of collective acres of plantings and water so the Willamette River almost overnight was barely worth hunting.

When the people pollution reached the point that to find a stool for a cup of coffee at Taylor's Drug Store in Independence was a "crap shoot", the time was at hand for remedial action. I sold the farm, loaded my decoys and paint brushes and, once again, headed up coast.

BLACK AND ATLANTIC BRANT

CHAPTER 6

Willapa Bay

WHILE STILL LIVING IN INDEPENDENCE, I had made several exploratory trips up coast as far as Willapa Bay. This estuary is tucked away in Washington's extreme southwest corner. The Columbia River on one hand and the Pacific on another. Jay Long knew the region well and we had dug razor clams there on a couple of occasions. These were winter trips so, of course, I did not overlook the wealth of waterfowl this almost pristine bay harbored. With this knowledge, it had to follow that my first landfall would be Willapa.

The Willapa River feeds into the bay's north end, and several others of lesser size feed in from the eastern and southern shores. All these streams have headwaters in the Coast range to the East. The narrow Long Beach Peninsula forms the western shore of the bay.

Willapa is a large bay, and still today supports one of the largest oyster cultures on the coast. Because of this industry, the water quality of the estuary has been jealously protected by the oyster men. Another factor in the preservation of the overall environment of this bay is that a large share of the total estuary acreage is a National Wildlife refuge. Yet, one other factor enters into protection for this pristine area which is the geographical remoteness of the place. So far, it is too far removed from "civilization" to have lured industry. Hopefully this will not change, but as the saying goes, "Anyone who believes that, stand on your head." At that time in the mid seventies, Willapa wintered a good population of black brant, and still does today—probably four or five thousand at least.

As I gazed out over the bay waters I almost swooned seeing all of those gorgeous brant. Not only was there a bundle of brant out there but, glory be, no hunters! (And I mean this almost literally). During the several years I lived on Willapa, I knew of only ten or a dozen guys who sought brant. There were some who hunted ducks, and many would come from afar to shoot the dusky Canada geese that wintered on the wildlife refuge but only a double handful went to the considerable effort it takes to successfully pursue sea geese. During my stay nothing changed this status quo.

My career as a sporting artist was, by now, firmly established and I did not have to work around the clock to make a decent living. As a result, I took advantage of my good fortune and hunted. Actually, the only curtailment was my physical stamina, and I had plenty back then. It was a good time, and I savored all that the bay had to offer along the lines of branting.

In the seventies, the brant limit was still at three birds, and the season was much longer than the present ten days. Most likely sixty days or more. In short order I figured out my favorite areas and techniques to hunt brant on Willapa Bay. A handful of locals hunted on the Ellen Sands in the northeast corner of the bay, but to get over there was a drive by car and boat trailer of almost sixty miles, or a boat trip across some ten miles of very unpredictable winter waters.

It didn't take a brain surgeon to figure out that there were a plenty of brant on my doorstep . I could hunt offshore a hundred or so yards by layout all up and down the west side of the bay. I could hunt from Otter Ridge, a sandbar, and with no need for a boat. Or, I could drive up the ocean beach and park my Scout and hike a mile or so to hunt another sand spit at Grassy Island. Again, with no need for a boat. The whole scenario was enough to boggle one's mind. Almost like owning a private brant club of several thousand acres! Not knowing, or caring why I deserved all of this, I simply gritted my teeth and dug right in. A majority of my hunts were just Lady and me. By now she was mature and knew the waterfowling drill well.

But in due course I met Joe Welch, who managed the Willapa Bay National Wildlife Refuge and who also enjoyed wildfowling. We soon became friends and hunting partners. At about the same time, I met Glen Noble, an unemployed renegade who lived solely to satisfy his two desires—to drink alcohol and kill waterfowl. He made no bones about the fact that his goal in life was simply to have fun. He received a monthly disability check from the government as he'd lost a finger during WWII while serving aboard a destroyer. Also his mother, who still lived in Illinois, sent him money. I don't know the amount in dollars from either source, but the total allowed him to follow a free soul life style. Glen hunted every day of the season. He had no boat or decoys, only his golden retriever, "Dingo" and his shotgun. It followed that with my boats and gear, Glen would now and again be my partner with about the same frequency as with Joe.

Joe and Glen had a great dislike for one another. Glen considered Joe a threat. Joe could arrest him for game violations—something at which Glen was an expert. Joe disliked Glen because he knew Glen was an inveterate game hog but neither he nor his staff were ever able to apprehend old Noble. It was, for me, a constant source of entertainment. Of course, we three never hunted together. When I hunted with Glen it was understood from the onset that I'd tolerate no "hanky-panky". And, by George, Glen honored this truce when with me, for the most part, at least. When I took Joe along we generally had a good time but somehow during the course of every hunt Joe would have to lecture me on the bad influence that Glen was bound to exert on my fifty year old being.

One day, Glen and I and our Goldens were set up with decoys on the bay's south end, rigged from a shore blind. Three mallards lit in and sat there in perfect range—all three heads up on necks stiff as pokers. Glen whispered, "I'll count to three, and we'll take 'em on the jump. OK?" "OK", I said. "One, two, BLAM!" Damned if the old coot didn't shoot all three ducks on the water with one shot. For the remainder of our days together—say several years, it was one of Glen's favorite jokes in mixed company. He'd poke me in the ribs and shout, "one, two, blam." Glen was strange.

Glen saved bands from ducks and geese he'd killed. Most guys who save bands are content to have them in a box in their den, on a string in their gear shed, or in some other place meant for memorabilia. Not Noble, he wore his around his neck

ONE, TWO --- BLAM!

as a lady would wear pearls. He wore them during all his waking hours. He also wore a shirt with all sorts of badges from hunt clubs back in Illinois and in the Sacramento Valley where he was a professional guide. I always felt that Glen should have been born about 1890 so he could have shot as many ducks as he wanted, and wherever.

Joe was not able to hunt so freely as Glen. Joe had a Federal job of great responsibility and a day off came infrequently. For Glen, every day was his oyster, so here was yet another bone of contention for Joe. It was hilarious for me standing there on the sideline.

Grassy Island protects the Long Beach peninsula's northern tip. It sorta hooks around into the bay and on the map appears as a cap on the peninsula. It is an island only by virtue of a tidal gut that is sometimes even wadeable. The island proper is not large, maybe twenty acres total: Sand, barely above high tides, with scrubby salt pines not more than fifteen feet tall. The tough native trees that can withstand a lot of abuse from horrendous winter storms that reach land at the Willapa bay jaws after blowing unobstructed across thousands of miles of Pacific Ocean.

To hunt brant at Grassy Island, I drove on the outer beach along the ocean up to the end of the peninsula. I had an International Scout then, and often a four wheel drive was a must on these beach runs. Once at the tip of the strand, I'd park the Scout up on the sand dunes above high tide and Lady and I would hike over to Grassy Island—about a mile. I had brant shadows stashed on the island year 'round. It took only minutes to rig about three dozen shadows and flags and the two of us would hunker down beside a huge fir log that had sanded in on a sand spit that connected to the east end of the island. I shot and Lady retrieved. We had a good many brant hunts on the spit at Grassy Island and never once did I meet another hunter during the years I gunned that spot. I know this sounds unreal in this day and age, but it is true. I'll wager that, still today, the spit at Grassy Island is a lonely place. Now and again we'd take a few ducks as well, but caution was the watchword as three brant and a limit of ducks became a weary load long before we reached the Scout over on the ocean sand dunes.

About three fourths of the way up the peninsula lies the tiny village of Oysterville. Some of the homes have dates posted on them, several of which are well over 100 years old. Not very old by New England standards, but out here on the Pacific, this is old! About four miles north of Oysterville was a break in the trees and brush alongside the gravel road named Stackpole. It was here I would park my Scout and head out afoot for some of the finest brant hunting one could hope for. In a northeasterly direction from the parking spot, about six-hundred yards out in Willapa Bay, lay a narrow sand bar some two-hundred yards long, by fifty yards wide. It had this dimension on an average winter daytime low tide. Between this bar and the peninsula, the water was shoal and the bottom hard sand. After some trial and error, I learned that by leaving the car about an hour before low tide I could wade to the bar in chest waders and get out there just as the spine of the sand bar showed above the surface. I carried thirty shadows and flags, an entrenching

tool, and a 4x4 tarp on a pack frame. My shotgun, I carried in hand. Lady swam alongside me as I slogged out in hip deep water toward the bar. Should the time of the low dictate that we leave shore in darkness, our course was easy to follow as the lights of the village of Bay Center across the bay were in direct line with the bar and the parked Scout. In daylight the village could be seen clearly over on the far side. If timing was figured correctly, we reached the bar as it came into view above the water's surface. First off, I'd put up the shadows and flags. By this time, the bar would have a good deal of surface above water and I'd start to dig a sit down pit. In other words, a shallow hole in the sand just large enough for my feet and deep enough for me to sit on the edge with my feet on the pit's bottom. (Like a chair.) Close around the pit were set six or more oversize shadows. These hid me when I crouched over with Lady lying on the sand alongside the pit. I always dressed in a black full length rain slicker to help with the camouflage.

My standard shotgun for this spot was my Dad's 870 Remington 12 gauge, a gun he bought new when this model came out in 1950, serial number 9370V. On this hunt there was no way to pamper any equipment, so I used only the 870. At the end of every hunt, the old pump would be bright orange with rust. In fact, one could watch it develop during the hunt. Sort of like a sun burn on unprotected skin.

I would guess, now in recall, that three quarters of my branting was done from Otter Ridge. This is the name I gave the bar one day when a large male river otter hauled up on to the bar not far from the pit, defecated, and at once slid back into the deep channel alongside the ridge and disappeared. He was out of the water only long enough for me to grab an idiot camera from my breast pocket and snap two pictures.

DECOYS RIGGED AT GRASSY ISLAND

Once the sand bar started to show above the lowering water the brant generally started to move down bay and past the set up. Some days they decoyed well and
then again on other days, showed no interest at all in decoys. One advantage of
Otter Ridge was the minimum amount of equipment needed to hunt it. If Joe or
Glen went with me, we shared the packing of the decoys.

Joe is short in stature and on some trips out to Otter Ridge, if we were pushing
the tide a little, the water would be close to the top of his waders. Always, Lady
swam along close by my side, looking up at me frequently, as if to say, "Hey man,
are we going to swim clear across the bay?" With nothing solid ahead in sight but
the far bay shore, I could understand her confusion.

Success on Otter Ridge did not always mean a limit of brant. Often, only a bird
or two. Now and then, zero. But icing on the cake out on Otter was the many other
species of birds that also used the bay. Shorebirds, ducks, eagles, falcons, and of
course, gulls and cormorants. Time passed quickly out on the Ridge, even when
the sea geese did not fly.

From my diary: December 20, 1978. Lady, Joe, Dave.
Set up on Otter Ridge – loads of birds flying – So. And
No. – Wind and rain heavy – 20-40 E - SE – most brant
I've seen in several hunts – had at least 60 birds in range
during the two hour low tide period. A great day. Bag- 6 brant.

Another day from diary: January 10, 1979. Lady, Joe,
Jack Brewton, Dave – Otter Ridge – Foggy with light
wind - West - switching to So. Lots of brant flew, but
in every direction but past the ridge. Just one of those
days, I guess. Bag- zero brant.

These two entries show the extremes of branting—feast or famine.

I've never felt that Joe fully enjoyed his hunts with me out on Otter Ridge, the
reason being that his only shotgun was a Winchester 21, 20 gauge. He'd sit on the
edge of the pit and watch . My "klunker 870" slowly change color from pitted gray
to burnt sienna. The sweat would break out on his brow—even on a cold day, and
feverishly he'd grab a special oiled rag he carried for these hunts and wildly start
rubbing down his baby. Often I suggested, even pleaded with Joe, to go over to
Astoria across the river and buy an old "beater" at the gun store. Hell, almost anything safe to shoot would have done the job and relieved the stress so he could
enjoy the hunt. But, he never did. Me, I just went home every night, steel wooled
the old Remington down and saturated her with WD40, stood her on her barrel
end to keep the solvent from running into the stock, and presto, there that pump
would be, ready and waiting to head out to Otter Ridge again. I have a bumper
sticker that reads, "My other gun is a Purdey."

Maybe I've said this before, but it bears repeating. Otter Ridge was tough on gear and body. There was no place to put anything down other than on the sand or in the water. Sure, I tried a small tarp to lay stuff on. Gun, etc., but the wind and moving feet of dog and man would soon have the tarp looking like the sand bar itself. In a boat or shore blind, things can be kept tidy and orderly. Not on the Ridge. I soon figured out that it worked well to lean my shotgun up against one of the shadows that circled the pit. This did not keep blowing sand out of the action, but did help some. I've had some experience with the traditional waterfowling guns, and I'll defend the Remington 870 as being one of the most dependable and resistant to foreign matter. This gun needs little pampering. In the long haul, Joe ended up holding his baby Winchester during the whole hunt. On windy days with the sand flying he'd even wrap his oily rag around the breech.

Down bay, near the town of Nahcotta, there stood an oyster landing handy to a large oyster bed. Many acres of oysters, owned by the Weigarts, I believe. In those years the oyster farmers did not object to our hunting on their leases. In fact, a couple of them suggested that I help myself to oysters for personal use if I chose.

It seemed that on a heavy east wind the brant moved along the west bay shore. Moved more predictably, that is. Glen had built a portable blind that was his pride and joy. It was a neat contrivance, I'll admit. It was an aluminum frame covered in gray canvas, very light weight and out on the bar, or on an oyster flat, it didn't seem to spook the birds at all. For the most part, Glen used this blind along wooded or grassy areas where there was some protection from the wind, as he'd made no provision to anchor it down. On this particular day we decided to hunt brant as a brisk Easterly was making up. We chose the oyster flat near Nahcotta since we could simply walk in there with no boat or wading necessary.

We rigged a bunch of shadows at the water's edge there on the mud with clusters of oysters all about us. The birds flew well along the flat and we got both brant and ducks. Dingo was doing his usual good job of retrieval so Glen never needed to leave his blind. There came a time, however, when Dingo had to go back up into the timber a hundred yards behind us to make a retrieve and for whatever reason in Glen's mind it was taking him too long, so Glen left his blind and headed back up to the woods with blood in his eye. The wind by then had kicked up pretty good and some of the gusts were worthy of notice. The blind stood firm at first, then shuddered a bit at the gusts , then in desperation just gave up and started to roll end over end, side over side, down the oyster flat toward the far horizons. The wind was actually out of the south east and the bar runs north and south so the blind took a course that would fetch it up against the

timber about three or four-hundred yards from our rig. Glen came out of the woods in time to see his blind well on its way to its final reward. He came storming up to me in a state of great agitation. Why didn't I grab the blind, why didn't I do this or that? Glen was some worked up. As calmly as I could, I replied , "Darn it, Glen, it just happened so fast. One moment the blind was there; I turned away for an instant, and ONE, TWO, BLAM it was gone and away down the flat." I don't remember that Glen told his favorite story about the three mallards again after that. Well, knowing Glen, maybe he did.!

> From my diary: Jan. 1, 1978 – Glen and Dave –
> Oyster Landing – Weigarts –Hunted out going tide
> with Glen's blockhouse blind. Wind heavy. S E showers.
> Lots of birds moving—Bag 6 brant –7 G. Scaup – 1 sprig.

Dingo was a great golden retriever. In some ways, that is. Glen got him as a pup and did a good job of training him to retrieve, but not so good in the minding department. Dingo did his own thing for the most part. A good share of the time he would not give up the bird, just stand there and growl and give you the evil eye. In time he'd put the duck down but Glen generally did not have the patience to wait Dingo out. So, often they had a set to and went at it. It was all very entertaining and , for me, so reminiscent of Joe and Couger. Dingo was from the strain of golden retrievers dubbed the " Peninsula Dogs". These goldens are deep red in color, tough, and well suited to the harsh winter conditions of Willapa Bay. Some of the males are Chesapeake-like in temperament. Dingo was one of these males. I got along just fine with Dingo. If he wanted to sit or stand around holding my

duck—so what. At least he didn't eat it like one "Chessie" I knew. My memories of
Dingo are good ones. He worked hard and we got along just fine with our under-
standing. Only when Glen was around was there conflict.

One day I launched my sneakbox over the oyster shell beach next to the old
Cannery in Oysterville. The plan was to row out about three-hundred yards offshore and rig up layout for bluebills and brant. This was generally pretty
productive and a nice change from the slog out to Otter Ridge. The morning was
clear with a steady southwesterly at about twenty. Enough to produce some chop,
but no problem weather-wise as the Peninsula gave some shelter if I didn't go out
too far into the bay. On these layouts I carried about twenty brant decoys on the
after deck and below, as well as a dozen drake bluebill blocks stored wherever I
could find room. I'd rig the decoys out there on lines of six or so to a string which
made it faster to pick up if it turned lumpy. This hunt was, as it turned out, one of
those I've dubbed "story book". A lot more birds than just brant and bluebills flew
that day. I'd rigged, by chance, in just about the main flight line of the flocks that
traded up and down the bay that morning. Scaup, wigeon, sprig, and even a few
mallards were moving, and in good numbers. The shooting was story book. Just
enough weather to make the day "duck-like"—whatever the devil that means. Bird
movement on a steady basis and of such variety to boggle the mind. I believe the
duck limit then was six—for brant it was three. In any event, when I rowed ashore
at the Cannery later that morning, there were three brant and a limit of ducks in
mixed species stashed neatly up under the bow of the sneakbox and the tide hadn't
changed but a foot.

One day Joe went out with me in my work skiff, an eighteen footer, to rig a net
blind offshore and hunt brant and duck. We used the sling launch at the Nahcotta

RIVER OTTER

boat basin and went up bay a half mile or so and out a quarter mile. We had an average hunt as my diary records, but it was special as Joe shot the largest brant either of us had ever taken. Joe had it weighed on the Ocean Park post office scale and this big male bird had a heft of over four and one half pounds! Not a record perhaps, but a great bird. Joe did some "basement" taxidermy and mounted the bird for his shop.

A bridge a tad over three miles long, spans the Columbia River between the Washington shore and the Oregon side in the town of Astoria. Nearer the Astoria side and just downstream from the bridge is a shoal area named the Desdemona Sands, which is only nine miles from the Pacific. A low tide at Desdemona Sands is virtually the same as on the ocean beach. At a certain stage on the low, these sand bars appear above the water and many species of birds gather there to loaf and preen. Gulls, cormorants, shorebirds, and yes, brant. On winter trips to and from Astoria, I'd see brant loafing on these vast sand bars now and again. It would take some figuring just how to hunt there and for sure it would be a crap shoot, but to an inveterate branter it had to be done. Weather would be a critical factor as the launch I'd use, the closest to the Sands, was still a couple of miles away. Anytime, but particularly in winter, the storms off the Pacific sweep in with such force as to make the Coast Guard choose the mouth of the Columbia as it's site for rough water boat training. I used my sneakbox to hunt the Sands and set shadows for the decoy rig. I sat among them just as I did on Otter Ridge with a pit. Now, so many years later, I do not remember how many hunts were made on the Sands. What I can recall very well is that I never shot or even saw a brant on any hunt. Being a slow learner, I likely made at least three hunts before giving up the program.

The Willapa River runs into the bay on the northeast corner. The town of Raymond is located on the river at its juncture with the bay. A state road runs along the shore here all the way out to the ocean to the village of Tokeland. Part way, along this road, the North River enters the bay. Here the State has constructed a very fine public boat launch. In spite of the fact that to trailer my sneakbox from the Peninsula to the North River was almost eighty miles, I would do so a couple of times each season for two reasons. The marshy area on the North River delta was much favored by wigeon, and I do personally favor wigeon. Besides a North River day was always a new scene, and the solitude in that small marsh was refreshing. Here again, as at Grassy Island, never did I encounter another gunner. A typical bag here would be mostly wigeon with a smattering of sprig, teal, and a bluebill once in a while.

The Naselle River, more like a good size "crick," enters Willapa bay in the southeast corner. Highway 101 crosses over a bridge at this junction of delta and bay. On the east shore is a sandy beach from which sturgeon fisherman fish from the shore. When the run is on some fish are taken. One day, as I drove past this beach, I noticed a few cars and pickups down on the shore and of more interest, a dozen or so people crowded about something at the water's edge. Being of a curious nature, I was forced to pull down to the river to poke my nose in. Once there I was overwhelmed at the sight of a monster white sturgeon at least eight feet long pulled ashore. Turns out some folks from out of state, Montana I believe, were fishing and had just gotten the brute ashore. Several local sturgeon fishermen also at hand were trying to convince the Montana folks that their fish was too big to legally keep. I got the feeling right off that the out of state folks were sure they were being flim-flammed, but at the same time were not really certain. Truth was, that at that time, sturgeon had to be 36 to 60 inches to be legal; under or over had to be released. As I drove away, the discussion was going on still and I've long wondered if some conclusion was reached before the poor fish expired out there on the beach.

Long Island occupies the lower one-third of the bay; is over six miles long and two wide at its fat part. The entire island is timbered with fir, hemlock, and cedar and is part of the Willapa National Wildlife Refuge. Hunting for bear, deer, elk and grouse is allowed in season by bow and arrow only. Long Island slough borders the island on the east and along the eastern shore of the slough is a good deal of tidal marsh. Few gunners used this area but many ducks did. It was an easy area to hunt but could only be reached by boat. At refuge headquarters at the south end of Long Island, the government had built a fine paved boat launch. From the launch up to the marsh was only a run of three miles in somewhat protected waters. This was not a marsh I hunted a lot, but for variety did so three or four times each season.

One hunt in particular comes to mind as unusual on this marsh. I'd gone out alone by sneakbox and carried only wigeon and pintail decoys as these species were most common there. The day was spring-like with the low tide in late morning.

VIEW FROM THE PIT — OTTER RIDGE

Generally my choice on a tidal marsh is to hunt the incoming tide for two reasons. Mainly, birds seem to work these marshes more on a flooding tide, and second, one can always be certain of getting out of the marsh again if one has been foolish enough to go into a shallow area on an ebb tide and get stuck. The flood will get you out! I was set up by mid morning but few birds were moving. As the tide made, some puddle ducks started working the marsh, but were above me at the north end. This went on for a time and soon caused me to wonder if I'd ever see any action where I'd rigged. Before long though, as the tide flooded the spot over my decoys, a few birds showed interest. Suddenly, as though a gate were opened, flock after flock began coming down slough from the north and started piling in the marsh and a good many all about me. Here again, I can't be certain of the limit then, but I believe it was six. Not that it would have mattered much time-wise if the limit had been twenty. There were ducks decoying steadily in range for at least fifteen minutes. As I shot at one bunch, another would be coming in. My guess now in recollection is that I brought to bag six birds in not more than three or four minutes—wigeon and sprig. As suddenly as this flight started, it stopped. I can only guess the reason, but suspect that the tidal movement prompted several thousand birds rafted up on the open water of the bay to all decide at once to come back to the marsh. Or possibly a crabber put the raft up and once awing they decided, why not just go to the marsh— it's about time anyway.

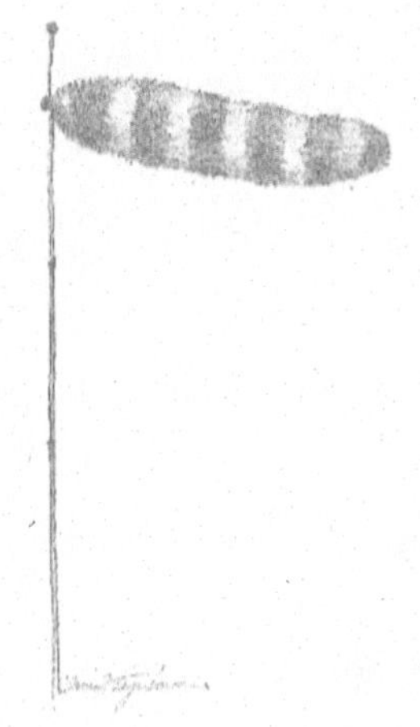

A good share of the time when Glen and I hunted together he would drive his pickup. Especially if we were not going to use a boat as his truck had no trailer hitch. Glen's truck was embellished with all manner of emblems and such. Sorta like Glen himself. You know, DU decals, bumper stickers that carried messages like "Game Cops Suck" or "I Love Ducks". His license plate said "FOWL" and a coon's tail was attached to each radio antenna. Glen knew how to live all right. Seldom did we not get some ducks. Not always a bundle, but few times less than three or four. No matter how many we'd bagged, the routine never varied for Glen. The birds were divided equally on two duck straps, you know the kind, tooled leather. One strap was hung over the rear view mirror bracket on either side of the pickup. His route now lay back to Ocean Park where he lived, but more specifically to Doc's Tavern where he could be found when not hunting. The ducks were now carried into Doc's and placed with great ceremony on the bar. After Glen was served a glass of wine, he launched into a detailed description of just how each and every one of those dead birds, still lying on the bar, met its fate. As a rule I ate no breakfast on an early morning hunt, so here was my chance for some leisurely bacon and eggs as Glen could really drag out a story. After I'd eaten and Glen was finished he would drive me home and return to Doc's for the day. The routine never varied when Glen drove his truck. When I drove, I simply dropped him off at Doc's on my way home. He lived only three blocks from the Tavern.

One of my dearest friends still lives in Ocean Park. Willie (Willard) Roeder, who is now pushing eighty. His wife, Lois, and his Golden, Tiger, are long passed on, but he still lives in their home of many years there on bay front. He and Lois

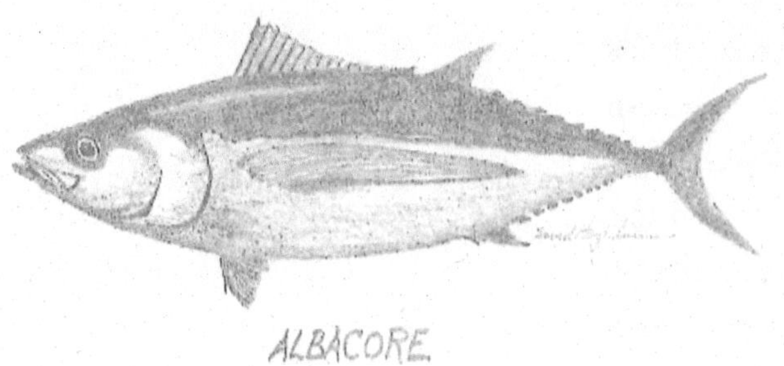

ALBACORE

owned and operated Lyle's Cannery, close by their home. I met these folks as I've long been addicted to smoked oysters. Lyle's turned out an alder-smoked oyster that had no equal. Smoked oysters were only a fraction of the Cannery's output. Canned sturgeon, salmon, and albacore made up the bulk of Lyle's business. In those years salmon fishing in the area was great and the various runs brought in anglers from all over. Many would drop their fish off at Willies and he'd smoke and can them on shares or by the case. During the busy season the little cannery hired several people to help keep up. Willie loves to hunt ducks, still does, so at once we hit it off. We'd hunt the bay front in front of his cannery or I'd take him out in the skiff to some marsh. Or, we'd hunt geese on a little club he belonged to down by Chinook. His Golden, Tiger, was another of the "Peninsula Dogs" but in Tiger's case his disposition was the exact opposite of Dingo's. Tiger was a natural retriever and was Willie's pride and joy. Willie told me recently that Tiger lived to be almost twenty years old! I still drive down to the Peninsula now and then to spend a day in the blind with Willie.

At the extreme south end of the bay is one of the refuge's public hunting areas. It is named the Lewis unit, and is comprised mainly of several fresh water lakes that are separated from the bay by a dike. This area got a lot of hunting pressure, as one could walk in after parking the car close by the lakes. I tried this a time or two, but the lack of quality hunting due to people pollution quickly turned me away. Old Glen, however, showed me that to walk way out on the dike could now and then produce some fast action on dusky Canada geese. Glen learned that the geese would transfer from bay to feeding grounds and then again back at somewhat certain times. A couple of occasions I went out on the dike with Glen and even got a goose or two but pass shooting holds little interest for me, never has, and that was that.

I cannot think of any waterfowling area that I've hunted where the American wigeon is a more important species than Willapa Bay. These delightful medium sized ducks have long been one of my favorites. Perhaps, if pushed, I'd have to confess that they really are the tops. I can't say exactly why, but suspect it is their eagerness to decoy, their excellence of flight, and beauty when in nuptial plumage and for me, not at all bad on the table. In any event, I love to hunt wigeon and seldom pass them up for other species; I may for a can or redhead or other somewhat uncommon species, but certainly not for mallard of sprig. Wigeon, for me, are flat out great ducks.

INTO THE RIG - SCAUP

DECOYING WIGEON AND SPRIG FILL THE SKY

Up along Willapa's west shore around Nachotta there were a lot of grass motts along the shoreline. I suspect this was the noxious spartina that now almost thirty years later is threatening the oyster culture on Willapa. Unaware of the threat that spartina grass was to become, I thought at that time what a great thing these clumps of grass were for the duck hunter. To hunt these motts, or clumps, was very simple. On a rising tide I would walk out across the firm sand/mud to a mott that was at waters edge, throw out five or six decoys and Lady and I would hunker down in the waist high grass. As the tide came in, we would eventually be forced to retreat back into shallower water taking the few decoys along to set out again alongside another patch of grass. At times the wigeon shooting from these grass motts was exceptional, but like all waterfowling, was never a lead pipe cinch. For me, gunning from the grass motts was just another way to hunt on Willapa to add variety.

On a hunt in the grass clumps one day, much to my surprise, a small band of white-fronted geese came over my hide, not twenty-five yards high. Luckily, I was looking up bay and saw them in time to get set. I was loaded with sixes, so a double was easy enough as the geese swept over. Speckle Bellies did not winter on our bay, but a good many came through on southern migration so to bag one was not all that uncommon.

The bay held a fair number of wintering canvasback ducks. At a guess, I'd say several hundred. They were not scattered all over the bay, however, and from what I could tell, concentrated in two locations. Scattered cans would be encountered just about anywhere but for the gunner who sought this species, like me, the places to go were Greenhead Slough, or right in front of refuge headquarters along the refuge line on Highway 101. Greenhead Slough formed in a tidal marsh that bordered Highway 101 on the southeast side of the bay. The slough then ran under a bridge and meandered on out into the main bay. There was a food source here that the birds sought and sometimes a hundred or more cans would be using Greenhead Slough not more than a couple of hundred feet west of the Highway 101 bridge. It was difficult to get a boat in the water here. There was no launch and the slough banks were mud, steep, and slippery. I did devise a method though to get at these cans. I still had the Ducker, and could easily slide it down the bank. Better yet I'd wait for the high tide, and thus have less slippery bank to contend with. The Ducker, a dozen can blocks, my shotgun, and some shrimp net and I was set. I did not take Lady on these hunts as space was minimal. A brief paddle of a hundred yards west of the bridge and the can area was reached. Sometimes the cans would be there, sometimes not, but it was always worth rigging out. The slough ran through a short grass marsh and the bank was steep. By net-

ting the Ducker over and tying her up close against this bank the boat and I were blinded effectively. The limit then was two canvasback ducks and as a rule, with patience, sometimes I would bag a brace of bulls. Other birds, of course, flew the slough and they were always fair game to me. The Ducker, as a blind, made for very cramped quarters so most often when I'd bagged my "trophy" birds, the hunt was over for me.

Near refuge headquarters, also right along Highway 101, was more short grass tidal marsh. Here again, the cans found something to their liking and on a rising tide would gather in numbers. No launch problem here, as the fine refuge boat launch was only three or four hundred yards from the "canvasback hole". It seems there is generally a problem of some sort and here it was the refuge boundary. The rather small area the cans favored straddled the refuge line and was also close by the highway. The refuge boundary was marked with big pilings so by lining them up there was no excuse to be in violation. Certainly here, of all places, one had to pay close attention. I liked this can "area" the best of the two—mainly because I could use my sneakbox, take Lady, and rig more decoys. A rising tide was always

best, in fact, when the tidal marsh was draining I never had any success. By launch-
ing the boat on the incoming tide, I'd row up close to the marsh. Here, it was great
to be able to row the short way and thus have the after deck free for the decoys.
Lady rode in the after part of the cockpit or on the bow deck, depending on the
water. Once at the marsh I would run the sneakbox up into a tidal gut and get as
close to the refuge boundary as possible. The decoys, usually eighteen or twenty, all
cans, were set on the grass to float later on as the tide flooded the marsh. The law
read that one could retrieve a downed bird from the refuge if one did not carry a
gun. So with Lady to retrieve any bird that dropped across the line I was in fat city.
The cans usually came into the flooding marsh from the open area so it was easy to
take them coming toward the refuge. Once the set up was worked out, it went like
clockwork. Frequently, one of the refuge staff or now and then Joe, would pull up on
the highway shoulder and shout out as to how was I doing. This was yet another
place on Willapa that never once did I see another gunner. As at Greenhead slough
there were other species coming in on the flood tide and with the sneakbox so comfortable I would stay longer and try for a larger bag. Now and then cans would

decoy along with wigeon or sprig so if two were in hand by then some care was needed on these mixed flocks. For whatever reason, Joe never once joined me to hunt cans at this great spot. On my home after these hunts I'd often stop at the refuge and give a hunt report for Joe to salivate over. What are friends for?

At Greenhead Slough and the Refuge Marsh, geese were common. The dusky Canada goose is a mid-sized race of Canada. Actually, there are two races—B.C. fulva and B.C. occidentalis. Both races are western and in fact, no further inland than the Willamette Valley. When I lived there the Valley was the southern limit of their range. On Willapa, a segment of the wintering flock of dusky Canadas stayed on and nested. I'm told this non-migratory flock is increasing. Many of these geese that stayed on, nested in the Greenhead Slough area and became almost like "golf course" geese in habit. At least it seemed to me that these birds seemed more trusting than most. They fly low about the marsh and bay and only on and around the public shooting units set aside by the refuge did they exhibit much wariness. To make a long story shorter, the geese I would take around Greenhead Slough or any other part of the bay for that matter, would seldom be more than thirty yards high. Never when I lived on Willapa bay did I hunt geese—meaning that no goose

decoys were rigged with goose hunting in mind. The dozen or so I shot each season were incidental to a duck hunt.

Along the eastern shore of the bay, three forks of the Nemah River enter the bay. The north and south forks don't amount to much, but the middle fork forms a very respectable tidal marsh of several hundred acres of short grass— possibly salicornia, but I am only guessing as I paid little attention back then to things botanical. On the south side of this marsh, a developer had started a "civilized" area. Lots were sold, people built homes, and a primitive boat launch was put in for access to the bay and marsh. Then, a locked gate was erected at the highway. Only residents and their guests had access. One of Joe's staff just happened to live in this development. How convenient! In due course, Joe had a gate key and the Nemah marsh was baptized. By this time, Joe had use of a Kennebeck sneakbox I'd given his son, Bill, as a graduation present. Although the launch was primitive it was okay for a sneakbox, and to hunt this marsh a boat was a necessity. So far as I was aware, the development launch was the only one of the marsh at that time. With such limited access, the place was just about not hunted. The Nemah marsh was little different from the other bay's marshes in either habitat or species. In other words,

WIGEON AND A CAN

DUSKY CANADA GOOSE

wigeon, sprig, teal, and now and then a mallard. For divers, bufflehead, goldeneye and a scaup now and then. In retrospect, I am certain today that the sole reason we hunted the Nemah marsh was because of the solitude, it was there, and it took a key to enter. Otherwise, it was just another marsh on Willapa where duck hunting was often very good.

Along the south shore of the Columbia River about four miles up stream from Astoria, Oregon, is the start of a marsh that is mind boggling in size. Most of it is the Lewis and Clark National Wildlife Refuge and in size it is roughly four by fifteen miles—all tidal marsh and islands—and almost all is open during season for waterfowl hunting! For me, it was an easy drive across the Astoria bridge and thence east on Highway 30 to a fine public boat launch on the John Day River about four miles above Astoria. I always used a sneakbox for my many hunts on this marsh. On this particular marsh one could encounter every species of waterfowl that used the Pacific Coast on migration. Predominate were wigeon, pintail, green-winged teal, and some mallards. Heading the diver list were scaup and canvasback. As always, were buffleheads and goldeneye. It followed then that my complement of decoys

114

was made up of several species. Here was the chance to really make a showing. My rig had wigeon and sprig—a dozen of each, half a dozen mallards, eighteen cans and bluebills—mostly drakes. The sneakbox carried fifty life-sized duck decoys easily as I had installed a bow rack. This marsh is so large that on days of poor visibility it was almost a certainty for me to get lost. One rule I quickly learned was to remember that the current flowed toward Astoria on the ebb and south was the Oregon shore. I always carried a compass in my shooting box.

The Lewis and Clark marsh had channels in a great variety of sizes. Some are so large and deep that even on low tides some gunning could be done. However, as with most coastal marshes the flooding tide was by far the most productive. The only problem I ever had in this marsh was trying to decide where to set up. There simply was too much of it. Like cereal or dog food on the supermarket shelves— which to choose? In time three or four areas became my favorites and always one in this small roster was right for whatever tide, wind direction, or other condition was at hand. Always, I kept my diver and puddler decoys separated. No matter that the species of either were mixed, that did not matter. Perhaps even mixing all would

not have mattered but it would have bothered me. It was unusual not to bag four or five species on this marsh on a single hunt. Areas in the marsh, especially around Russian Island contained little "villages" of float camps. Many of the Astoria duck hunters built these for their seasonal pleasures. A typical float house or duck camp would be 14x24, one room, maybe two, frame construction, metal roof, a four foot deck all around, and floatation would be cedar or fir logs. Big logs. Some three to three and one half feet in diameter and forty feet in length. Today, these would be worth a small fortune. Some of these camps were left anchored in the marsh all year. Others were towed by their owners back to town or other safe moorage for the off season. In due course, I met several of these "marsh rats". All were serious waterfowlers. Most were hospitable and few resented my being in the marsh as a freelancer. Many, if not all, showed great interest in my sneakbox and it struck me that few had ever seen one before. These guys all came to the marsh by larger craft Some towed gunning skiffs, some kept these skiffs on the float house deck when they were away. One float house I visited had a special "garage" on one end that housed the gunning skiff and decoys. Most of the gunning skiffs I examined were of the local "Astoria design", double ended, poled or round and most designed for one gunner, dog, and decoys. Some of these river hunters also built duck boats and carved decoys. These carvers and boat builders made decoys and skiffs for those less talented and were always busy. This is true nationwide, of course.

FLOATHOUSE - RUSSIAN ISLAND
COLUMBIA RIVER ABOVE ASTORIA

The Astoria region has produced several decoy carvers of renown. The most notable of this group was undoubtedly Chas. M. Bergman. Sometimes he was referred to as the old man or grand old man of the "Astoria Group." Bergman came from Finland, but was Swedish. During his life in Astoria, he was a commercial fisherman and boat builder. Today Bergman decoys are much sought after by collectors. Likely the most sought after of any Northwest carver. Other carvers of the Astoria Group are Frank Bay, Oscar Hendrickson, John North, Chas. Pice, and James Titus, just to name a few. It is interesting to note that decoys made by the Astoria Group, for the most part, show the "Bergman Influence", and Bergman decoys, in turn, show the Mason Decoy Company influence.

Late one season, the idea came to mind that a "pure" diver hunt in the Russian Island area would be a change of pace. Cans and bluebills were there on every hunt I'd made and as I always took pot-pouri the divers made up a minor part of the bag. Sprig and wigeon were predominate so my decoy rig favored those species. What a great variety to rig a spread of canvas back and bluebill decoys and shoot only those two species—drakes only. Many times these plans to make "special" hunts with rules that are overly restrictive result in big disappointments; now and again, not. By choosing a day with a mid-day high tide I figured to have the maximum hours of good bird flight. All seemed in order, my homework was well done and with spirits high, I set out for the boat launch on the river over on the Oregon side. With the sneakbox in the water, and the truck parked, I waded out to start the engine and stood alongside while the Evinrude fifteen warmed up. This was standard procedure for me as far back as I can remember. Comforting to know the engine will keep running when you climb into the boat, throttle back to idle to shift into gear, rather than having to restart as river current or tide carries you and the boat in an unwanted direction. This day the venerable old fifteen had the bit in her teeth and balked to beat the band. Being careful not to flood her, I pulled over and over. I checked the gas tank vent, the fuel line connection at the tank and at the engine. Pulled the hood and checked plug wires. No gas fumes to indicate flooding. Now, what the devil! In time, I simply gave up, took the outboard off and locked it in the truck. I started as a waterfowler who rowed where the hunting was. By "Jimminies", I could do it still.

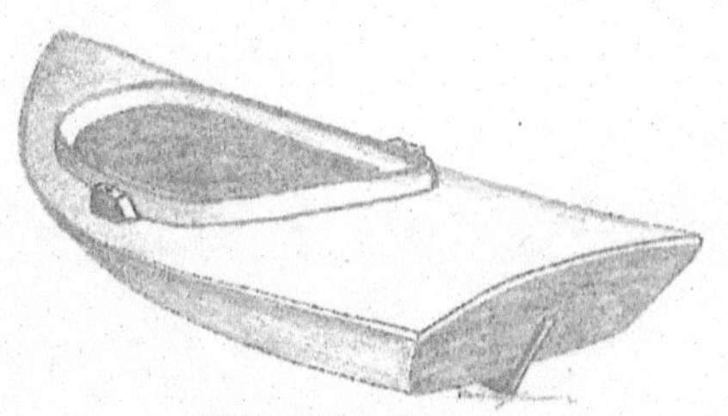

GUNNING SKIFF BY
SVEN LUND · ASTORIA · CIRCA 1970

A short ways down the river and on out into the marsh is a very large grassy island that has a small bay on the westerly side with a hook at the bay's end—sorta point-like. Quite suddenly, a five mile row up to Russian Island didn't seem like a

OSCAR HENDRICKSON   1880·1953
FRANK BAY· 1896·1980
JOHN NORTH   1886·1945
CHAS. M. BERGMAN - 1856·1946
JAMES E. JENSEN -(UNKOWN)
JAMES TITUS, SR. - 1879·1956
MASON DECOY FACTORY
1896 - 1924
LOWER COLUMBIA
RIVER CARVERS.
CHAS. A. PICE - 1890·1958

great idea for a couple of reasons. Five miles up there was one thing, but it follows, as always, that it would be five miles back. Secondly, the prediction on the weather station that morning was pretty serious about some wind later in the day. As I mulled over these facts, the small bay with the grassy point sounded better and better and it lay only over a mile from the boat launch. The die was cast, and I rowed off towards the little bay.

By the time I reached the bay I was about an hour late tide-wise, but nothing could be done to change that. The tide was making at a good clip as I set the decoys behind the small point. To draw attention to my rig which was sort of hidden, I set four or five blocks out a bit off the point with another handful leading back toward the main spread in a loose line. Once the decoys were out, I hastily snugged the sneakbox up against the sheer bank and threw the shrimp net over her. No need here to fool with grass and such.

By now the promised wind was picking up and off to the west and north I could see white horses starting to build. Good. Birds rafted out there would be fools not to seek some comfort back here among the islands. In particular, my little bay that so far was about as serene as could be. During the decoy rigging and netting the boat, only scattered birds were to be seen. Certainly not enough to get a guy all fired up. The wind kept building, the tide kept flooding, and coinciding with these two natural forces, the ducks got to moving. All species of puddlers, and in numbers that would have made Glen Noble get all choked up! The temptation was almost more than a body can bear not to take these sleek bull sprigs and those big old green heads. Not to mention the wigeon and teal. There was hardly a time that there was not some sort of duck or ducks sitting nervously out there among the blocks. But here I was, bound to take only divers—scaup and or cans in particular. Both these species were awing, but so far paid little to no attention to my spread. The handful of blocks I'd set out off the point were in such rough water by now that they could barely be made out. The white of the wave crests looked so much like the white of the can decoys that as attractors they were virtually worth-

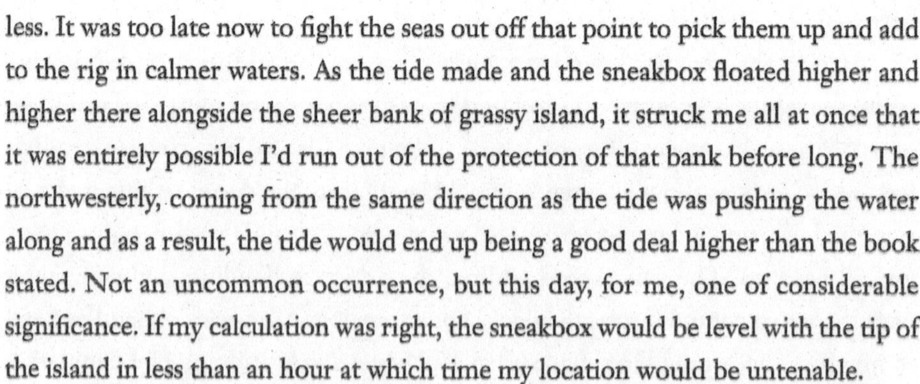

less. It was too late now to fight the seas out off that point to pick them up and add to the rig in calmer waters. As the tide made and the sneakbox floated higher and higher there alongside the sheer bank of grassy island, it struck me all at once that it was entirely possible I'd run out of the protection of that bank before long. The northwesterly, coming from the same direction as the tide was pushing the water along and as a result, the tide would end up being a good deal higher than the book stated. Not an uncommon occurrence, but this day, for me, one of considerable significance. If my calculation was right, the sneakbox would be level with the tip of the island in less than an hour at which time my location would be untenable.

A decision needed to be made at once. Stay a tad longer and hope for a diver, or get the hell under way. To my credit, I choose the latter and threw the netting aboard, picked up the blocks, wisely storing them under the decks for flotation—you see, I hadn't forgotten the Big blow at Netarts! Once all was in order I started the haul towards the John Day river mouth. The wind was only partly abeam as I rowed on a course for the river and so long as I pulled hard to keep steerageway all went well. It was no big deal, and shortly we were in the protected water of the river. A short pull of ten or so minutes and the boat launch lay dead ahead. Once the bow scratched up on the bar alongside the ramp I hunkered down over the oars and the truth slammed into me—I had not fired one round! Not a single shot had I taken on this all fired great diver hunt I'd dreamed up! This in itself was bearable but the visions of those sprig, mallards, wigeon, and teal in and out of the decoys earlier would nag me for days. Once I caught my breath my composure also seeped back. I'd made it hadn't I? Went through the motions, did it all correctly, what matter indeed that the divers never showed over the blocks. Just being amarsh, out there on such a wild and hairy day would remain in my recall longer than a bag of bluebills. By the time the sneakbox was trailered and I was across the Astoria bridge towards home, whatever disappointment bugged me earlier was a thing of the past. First though, the old Evinrude had to be taken in for repair tomorrow before anything else. Turned out the magneto on the fifteen was out. Oh yes, and I named the little bay "Best Laid Plans Cove." Don't bother to look, you'll not find it on any chart.

CHAPTER 7

Skagit

N ONE BEAUTIFUL WARM DAY IN MID JUNE, 1979, my wife, Delphie, and I pulled into the small channel town of LaConner, Washington. Actually, we were en route to Sequim in search of a new abode. We had heard that the town of Sequim on the strait of Juan de Fuca was quite dry with as little as 15 or so inches of rain per year. Our stop in LaConner was mostly just for lunch. We were at once taken with the quiet atmosphere along the main street on the waterfront. There were even plenty of parking spaces! As one, we agreed that to leave this place without further investigation could well be a grave mistake.

After but a few inquiries as to rentals in the area, we were told by a shop owner, a Mrs. Earp (yes, a descendant of the famous Wyatt) that there may be a rental in a new development called Shelter Bay just across Rainbow Bridge. We found the real estate office adjacent to the Marina where we met a young Don Zimmer. Don told us there were no rentals in Shelter Bay but three houses for sale. We looked at two which raised no interest, but the third one struck a chord in us both. It was not officially on the market but Don gained entrance for a quick look see anyway. Liking what we saw in the fast walk through, we repaired back to LaConner for lunch and some deep thinking regarding the purchase of a new home.

A seafood lunch and two martinis later, we were back in the Shelter Bay realty office putting earnest money on our new digs. Problem number one was at once at hand as the owner would be unable to vacate for about six weeks. This did not faze us in the least. We took a "suite" of rooms at a Burlington motel called the Mark II—a popular overnighter for cross country truckers. Our two rooms were on the second floor, the top, and in the summer of 1979 with heat records being set almost daily, we wondered at times if this all had been such a good idea. In time, however, six weeks of it to be exact, we were finally moving into the new digs. It was a new home that kept us anchored in one place for twelve years.

By the time we were established in the new home in Shelter Bay, waterfowl season was at hand. In those years the brant season coincided with the duck season. However, Washington's duck season traditionally opened on the second Saturday

of every October, so early on in the Fall very few, if any, brant were yet on the bay. Mid November, I quickly learned, was plenty soon enough to start going out for sea geese.

Shelter Bay is on Fidalgo Island and separated from the mainland and LaConner by a channel of navigable water. Still called "the slough" by many older residents, this channel is dredged when necessary to maintain a depth that will accommodate larger fishing vessels and yachts of plus one hundred feet.

The Swinomish Indian Reservation constitutes most of Fidalgo Island. Shelter Bay's four hundred and some acres are leased from the tribe with the exception of forty some acres of fee simple land on which our home was located. The west end of the channel enters Skagit Bay and the Northern end enters Padilla Bay. Shelter Bay has a well kept marina with access into the channel. At the time I had a four-teen-foot Gregor skiff that proved adequate for most days on both bays weatherwise. I also had the Barnegat bay sneakbox from earlier years. So, from the marina which was barely a half mile from the house, I could crab, clam, duck and

brant hunt on either bay or the delta of the Skagit river's North Fork.

Down channel toward Skagit Bay, the waterway makes an S curve between the two rocky headlands of a Shelter Bay promontory and McGlinn Island. This curving narrow passage is called Hole in the Wall. At the S curves, beginning on the right was a tiny water front cluster of boat houses, sheds and two float homes. Locally known as Frog Town, the "community" had only one resident when I arrived on the scene. His name is Ed Houck and he presently resides in Sedro Woolley. Ed is about my age and we hit it off at once. In 1979 he and his wife, Betty, had a home in Sedro Woolley, but almost weekly would take a skiff and row from LaConner down to Frog Town and spend a couple of days and nights in the two bedroom float house—one of two that Ed owned there. One day, Delphie and I interviewed and taped a lengthy conversation with Ed. He revealed that he had been born in Frog Town circa 1920, and went to school in LaConner via rowboat. His father and uncle built boats and fished commercially for salmon all from the Frog Town base. At one time, Ed related, Frog Town had sixteen residents. It's largest population ever. As late as the late sixties, Frog Town had no electricity. A Mr. Gene Dunlap and Ed made a deal. Ed built a rowing skiff for Dunlap in exchange for an electric line run from Dunlap's home on the bluff in Shelter Bay above Frog Town, down to Ed's boat house. The story goes that Dunlap, then in his seventies rowed all the way around Fidalgo Island in one day in the skiff that Ed had built. Delphie and Lady and I went to Frog Town often to set crab traps, picnic on the deck of the boat house or on the wharf in front. Sometimes Ed would be there, sometimes not. He had given us permission to use the place as we chose. In time, the smaller of the two float homes took my fancy. Ed did not use it and the

125

notion struck me that I needed a shanty over in the delta marsh of the North Fork of the Skagit River.

By this time Tom Newell and I had done a good deal of hunting in the marsh and each time we did, we'd bemoan the fact that we had no duck camp. After devising many imaginary camps from tents to building our own float house, we agreed that asking Ed if he'd sell us his spare house (the one bedroom model) was the most intelligent first course of action. In due course, I had the chance to discuss this purchase with Ed and he was at once agreeable to the transaction. His only reservation was what did I plan to do with it. When I told him it was to be a duck camp he was most pleased and said that it was a fitting end for the home to be residing over there in the marsh in the shadow of Bald Island. The time had come for my question. "What are you asking for her Ed?" After a lengthy silence Ed asked ,"Do you think five hundred is fair?" Being prepared for a much healthier figure I assured him it was more than fair. Tom, of course, would share with me the purchase price, so there was no need for either of us to "mortgage the ranch."

Now comes the "nitty-gritty". The shanty, 12 x 18 feet in size sits on cedar logs, some three feet plus in diameter, and 24 feet in length. These logs had been under the float house since 1934 when the place was built. Red cedar is highly water resistant and lasts for years. The house resided in tide waters and would float on high tides and the logs rested on the mud at low tide. This in and out of the water every twelve hours, Ed explained, allowed the logs to "drain" a little on each low tide and thus retain some buoyancy. Not much, but enough to keep the Shanty afloat—barely.

The house was surrounded by six to eight inch diameter pilings that the Houck's had hand driven decades earlier. Tom and I worked on low tides for the better part of a week to remove the some dozen and a half pilings so the house could be towed out into the channel. Salt water had virtually petrified some of these pilings making them impossible to cut. We proved this to our satisfaction by ruining two chain saw blades! These rock hard pilings had to be dug out! Eventually, the chore was done. Before moving, however, the float house needed more floatation to insure a safe passage down channel, around Goat Island, and up the Skagit River to the Bald Island slough.

Jim Suomela, a good friend down in Pacific County, was fishing commercially in Alaska. When he was home in Ilwaco, we'd get to hunt now and then. I just knew Jim would be more than willing to become a third partner on the Shanty venture. His "investment" was to be several billets of styrofoam, the kind used under many floating docks. This foam is of the closed cell type and lasts virtually forever. Jim delivered the billets on his flatbed truck, Tom and I installed it under the Shanty decking during two or three low tides. Once under, aiding the ancient cedar logs, we gained about four inches of "freeboard"—enough we felt to insure safe passage over to Bald Island. Even I knew that moving the Shanty would require the services of a tugboat of some sort. With some reservation, I called the office of Dunlap Towing Company based in LaConner. They treated my request for this

towing job with as much courtesy as they would have for a tow job to Japan! A Mr. Max Robinson was assigned the tow, and he was to drive the Uff Da, one of Dunlap's smaller tow boats. Max advised us which tide would be best—a very high one, as the site we'd chosen was on high marsh ground owned by Charles Leibst of Seattle. Our rent was free so long as we "reported" to Mr. Leibst each year and related to him how the duck hunting had been and if we still enjoyed our camp site. Some fine landlord, eh?

On the appointed day, an hour or so before the high tide, we met Max at Frog Town in the Gregor skiff. Tom was along and would follow us down channel and upriver as Delphie, Lady and I rode on the Shanty's fore deck on beach chairs. We could have ridden back to town on the Uff Da but we wanted to spend the day securing the duck shack to willows until the time we could get at hand setting some pilings. Max secured his towline to the logs under the deck of the Shanty's front

porch and slowly he eased her out into the slough and toward Hole in the Wall.

Of great concern to Delphie was a nest of barn swallows under the eaves of the Shanty on the back end. The young could not yet fly, so it was up for grabs just what the parents would do—abandon the chicks or follow our progress over to Bald Island. Some years earlier when I lived in Independence and rode the "Bueny" ferry across the Willamette, frequently I was always enthralled to watch the several pairs of swallows that had nests under the eaves of the ferry's wheel house and in the four inch tubing hand rails. These birds followed the ferry back and forth across the river as a matter of course. Therefore, my vote was that the Shanty swallows would follow us over to Bald Island and accept their new habitat with no fuss. Fortunately, for my sake, the swallows did exactly as I predicted and Delphie was not forced to leave me as she'd threatened had the swallows abandoned their young.

As Max and the Uff Da towed the float house down the channel, pleasure boaters passing our flotilla did considerable neck turning while they gazed in amazement as we proceeded at two knots or less toward Goat Island where Max would turn South, circle the island and thence head up the Skagit River toward Bald Island. At the Island he turned into the slough and proceeded to the site that Charles Leibst had so generously loaned us. Once there, Max unhitched the tow line, pushed the Shanty around so the front porch faced the slough, and then simply pushed it back into a gap in the willows where it sits to this day over fifteen years later.

As it turned out, the pair of barn swallows that so faithfully followed the Shanty from Frog Town to Bald Island returned each summer for at least four years to raise their young in that same nest under the eaves.

We hand set the six to eight inch spruce pilings that Jim supplied as a sort of bulkhead between the slough and shanty. These formed a barrier to prevent drift logs from piling up in our "front yard". Two were also set on either side of the house to moor to. That same summer during a rise in the river I snagged a very decent float about 10 x 18 inches in size that had broken loose from someone's river front lot upstream and fetched up in the willows out on the river downstream of the island. As I towed it down the slough with my skiff, I could'a recited TWAIN'S book HUCK FINN by heart. It took me back a lot of years to my youth on the Mississippi only twenty miles upstream from Hannibal, Missouri where friend Huck lived, made rafts, towed floats, and all manner of such good stuff.

By early Fall and with the duck season at hand, we had our duck camp ship shape. We hauled stove wood over by the skiff load and quickly had a winter's supply ricked up on the side deck and in the kitchen's corner by the stove. In the bedroom we built a couple of bunks in a tier. The toilet room that for years had simply emptied directly into the water below now held a new porta potti. (EPA approved!) Our kitchen sink, however, drained directly into the marsh below but never once did I hear any complaints from the muskrats, beaver, mink, otter, or coyotes that shared the marsh with us.

Tom and I had hunted the immediate area for two seasons prior to the introduction of the duck shack, so were very familiar with the areas that produced the best hunting on any given tide and or weather. At this time there were a lot of greater scaup in Dunlap Bay, not more than four hundred yards from our camp. A deep channel ran through this small bay almost it's entire expanse. The channel provided access to the bay/marsh even on a low tide. A small island at the channel edging about half way into the bay provided the site we needed for superb bluebill hunting. The wintering flock that used this little bay numbered perhaps three hundred birds. By not shooting too frequently, say once a week, we would enjoy consistently fine scaup gunning. The birds would come into this marsh to feed on very small seeds from a marsh grass of which I no longer recall the name. As the tide rose, the bluebills would fly up the channel towards the flooding marsh beyond. They came in dribbles of a couple or three to small flocks of ten or fifteen. The whole lot never came at once. We'd rig a couple or three dozen bluebill decoys along the outer edge of the Island, grass our sneakboxes over and tie up along that same edge. I can only say that we enjoyed bluebill gunning the likes of I've never had better before or since. As the years passed, the greater scaup numbers using Dunlap Bay dwindled and the flock that today uses the Eastern side of

Padilla Bay has grown considerably. I can only surmise that for whatever reason only scaup understand there is better chow on Padilla Bay. At the time of this writing, friends who still hunt Dunlap Bay for puddlers tell me that very few bluebills use that marshy bay.

When Tom and I hunted puddlers in Dunlap Bay we always used a certain spot that suited exactly our method. A deep, but narrow channel ran into the short grass marsh and at the entrance to this channel rested a large root ball from a giant fir tree. A hundred feet or less up the channel rested another piece of drift. Our plan dictated our arrival on this spot be when the solid marsh ground with its covering of short grass was still high and dry. An hour or so before the rising tide covered it was ideal. We'd set a couple of dozen shadows, sprig, mallard, and teal in the grass and a couple or more dozens of full bodied floater decoys interspersed among the shadows with the anchor and line of each decoy lying along side on the mud. Our sneakboxes would be grassed over and one tied alongside the two drift logs. Tom shoots from his port side so he got his choice of location which varied as did the wind. I shoot from either side, so it mattered little to me. I can miss from one side as well as the other. Once settled into our boats we were set for several hours of uninterrupted hunting with no need to fool with decoy changes. Both the shadows and floaters were working for us before the tide covered the grass. Once it did, the

  SHADOWS IN GRASS IN DUNLAP BAY

DAVE HAGERBAUMER
VENA VISTA, OR. 1972
HOLLOW CEDAR

TOM NEWELL
GIG HARBOR
HOLLOW CEDAR
1996

HAGERBAUMER
BURLINGTON 1993
HIGH DENSITY CORK

HAGERBAUMER
LA CONNER 1981
SKAGIT MODEL
HOLLOW CEDAR

HAGERBAUMER
HIGH DENSITY CORK
1996 MODIFIED BLUNT TAIL

HAGERBAUMER
BURLINGTON 1996
HIGH DENSITY CORK
BLUNT TAIL

David Hagerbaumer

HAGERBAUMER
PATTERN AND BODY
NEWELL HEAD AND PAINTING
HIGH DENSITY CORK 1990

MODERN CUSTOM BILT DECOYS
BY NEWELL / HAGERBAUMER

HAGERBAUMER
HIGH DENSITY CORK
1990

shadows were under water but the full bodied decoys were floating and doing their job. On days when the birds were flying well, we would sometimes have limits before the marsh flooded. It would be a snap then to walk about among the stool and gather them all from solid ground. More often, we'd hunt long after the shadows had gone under. Once this happened it became imperative to wait for the tide to fall enough to expose the shadows so we could find them. .

Dunlap Bay, on the other hand, was only one of many places that Tom and I hunted in the shanty area. Tom lived in Gig Harbor then and still does—a two and one half hour drive to LaConner. As a result he was unable to get into the marsh only a fraction of the times as I did. Lady was in her prime when I started gunning up in the LaConner area, so she always accompanied me in the sneakbox with the exception of when I laid out in open water for divers or brant. I feel a dog is a liability when gunning from a float or a boat in open water. Decoy lines, tidal currents, eelgrass, and winds all combined are a recipe for a disaster for the dog. Some will disagree, I'm certain, but better safe than sorry as the time honored saying goes.

A small island stands guard over Skagit Bay alongside the channel that comes through Hole in the Wall. This was the island I called Goat Island in my narrative

on moving the Shanty from Frog Town to Bald Island. Why it has the name of Goat Island I do not know, but another name used commonly hereabouts is Fort Island. This name makes sense, as atop this little island during World War II, our government had installed a five inch rifle in a concrete position. Dozen of such gun sites were put in early in the war in hopes of defending our narrow Puget Sound waterways against submarine and surface attack against shipping and naval shore installations.

We have friends who bought one of these concrete bunkers and refitted it into a home. Imagine a home with a three foot thick roof! No leaks, you can bet. Their view is spectacular. From their home site high up on a hill one can see the Pacific Ocean at the mouth of the Strait of Juan de Fuca and to the East, the Cascade mountain crest. The distance combined of a hundred fifty miles. And across the strait, Vancouver Island and the Capitol of British Columbia, Victoria, Jewel of the North West.

Along the base of the Island on the Skagit Bay side is a flight lane for divers. Scoters and goldeneyes in particular. Many is the time I threw out ten or a dozen sea duck decoys, anchored the Gregor or sneakbox and just waited, no blind needed. The birds would come from either direction and if I'd set the stool just right, most would fly right over the rig. I broke my own rule here and took Lady as these were protected waters and solid ground was only a stones throw off. I had rigged a modified ladder, the kind made for water ski boats. On mine, I'd attached a piece of half inch plywood 18 x 18 inch in size to the bottom of the ladder. When lady swam up to this platform she'd get her "hinders" set on the board eight or ten inches under water and put her "fronters" up on the top of the gunnel and I'd help her climb over. Sometimes with a duck, but always with a gallon and a half of water!

The Skagit Bay foreshore on the east side all the way from the river's North Fork, south to the delta of the South Fork is a distance of roughly ten miles. This entire stretch of foreshore is littered with hundreds, maybe thousands of logs and stumps. Some are entire trees with the root ball still attached that have toppled into the river and floated down to the river's twin deltas only to fetch up in the foreshore's short grass marsh. A combination of extreme high tides in company with heavy onshore winds, deposit these stumps, logs and trees far up on the shore where they sand in and become almost permanent fixtures of the marsh edging of the bay. Waterfowl become used to these fixtures and pay little or no attention to them. So, it follows that water fowlers use these logs and stumps as ready made blinds, and most of the foreshore's gunners have their favorite hides. As a season draws on and nears the end, the wintering fowl seem, to me, to become a bit leery of these stumps and tend to shy away.

In my early years of gunning the Skagit marsh, I also took advantage of these logs and stumps and would tie my sneakbox alongside one and become virtually invisible. With a rig of decoys properly set, this was a deadly set up—particularly during the early season. In fact, I carried aboard my sneakbox, as standard equipment, a hammer, some twenty penny nails, and some dogs to tie my sneakbox to on logs with no limb stubs. Gradually I'd decorated so many logs and stumps with dogs and nails that after several seasons there was no longer need to carry the hammer and nails. As time went on, I got the feeling that some birds did indeed shy away from stumps and logs—all the time. This prompted me to start laying out in the short grass marsh, in open water, the sneakbox netted and grassed over, and two or three confidence gulls on the decks. With thirty or so decoys properly set this method was almost sure fire and quickly I never tied up to logs in the future. Using this rig, I was able to get off by myself and eliminate the marsh cowboys who had no compunction about taking a log close by one who had been there first and had already set up his decoys. Yes, there are those "sports" who love to snuggle up to an other's rig of decoys and "share" the shooting with the unfortunate guy who tries to do it right.

The foreshore marsh at low tide was solid ground covered with several varieties of marine grass. For the most part, short stuff with clumps of taller growth scattered about. The tall growth, mainly cattail, willows, and a head high grass that reminded me of canary grass that I had on the farm in Oregon. All this taller growth made for fine ready made blinding, but here again, I do feel some of the more astute birds were leery of it in time.

Very few birds used the marsh at low tide as the only water was that in the ditches, guts, and "dreens" that laced the area. The seeds the fowl sought were more readily available to the dabblers when water flooded the short grass.

Ideally, I chose to be on the marsh as the tide was incoming and starting to flood the guts and drains (dreens). I'd follow one of these guts into a vast open area, an area with no stumps or logs of any real size. Once on site, I'd tie the sneakbox to an oar jammed into the firm mud and proceed to set my decoys on solid ground. As the tide made, it gradually began to cover the ground where the decoys sat strand-

Mallards Alarmed

ed. All this while, I had been arranging the shrimp netting over my sneakbox and applying a liberal covering of the same grass that grew alongside the drains. Once the boat was grassed, I repositioned it just so and this time re-anchored it fore and aft with ten pound navy tape. Both anchor lines had small floats attached to the end that snapped to the bow of the boat and transom. A light line was attached to each float to keep the whole rig one piece. With this anchoring system it was simple to unsnap the bow and stern and row out to retrieve downed birds when Lady was not along. It was just as simple to snap back up as the tide continued in, the short grass was, in time, almost covered. At this point, the grassed over sneakbox was just another grass clump out there among a thousand others. Only this one had a couple of gulls on it—a common sight in that marsh. Or, at times my faithful heron decoy made in 1971.

I'd say that laying out in the foreshore marsh was by far my favorite method of hunting this particular habitat. And, back there in the generally protected waters, Lady was a great helpmate and saved me a lot of snapping and unsnapping of anchor lines.

One hunt in particular comes to mind when writing about layout. Tom was up

and the two of us chose to shoot the open marsh across the river from Bald Island. We rigged our decoys, using those we each carried to form one big spread. We set our boats side by side with Tom on the right so he had full swing from his port side. Both were grassed over and we settled down to wait. It turned out to be one of those special days when new birds were arriving in the marsh. I felt that I could always distinguish these new migrants because they responded so eagerly to calling. Earlier, arrivals seemed to be bored when one called. I'm referring now to mallards. Anyway, we had a great time. The birds came to the calling and the decoys just like it says they should in Ralf Coykendall's book *Decoys and How to Rig Them*. Perhaps I jest—but it is a fun book to read and indeed a classic.

After a time the wind picked up and by the time we had plenty of birds it was evident that picking up the decoys would be a workout. In these shallow grass choked waters the use of the outboard was nothing but a headache. So, we rowed up to the upwind end of the rig and grabbed as many decoys as possible, then got blown back down through the rig. We'd throw out the anchor and sort out the decoys and wrap the lines in a figure eight around the body with two or three wraps around the neck. Anchors were unsnapped and thrown into the open anchor bag. Then we pulled the anchor and rowed back up to the head of the spread and started all over. In due course we got it done. On this particular day we had both got blown through the rig and thrown out our anchors about the same time. Most of the blocks were aboard and we were taking a blow when along came a bull can decoying to the double handful of decoys still out. Tom and I have always chosen not to load our shotguns until our rig is set and we are ready to hunt. The last thing we do is uncase our Brownings and load them. The same goes when the hunt is over—only in reverse. Shotguns are unloaded and cased—then we start taking off grass and nets then picking up decoys. So here we were, guns unloaded and cased as the bull can approached—the first and last we would see that season. The old brute dragged the decoys and circled way out and came back to do it all over again. And, by Jimminies, he did it a third time before departing into the haze out over

MALLARDS IN THE FLOODED TIMBER

the bay proper. We would have had plenty of time to uncase a gun, load and likely have bagged that can between us, but I'm very proud to say that neither of us made a move to do it. Old, but safe habits are hard to break.

Another time we were set up for teal on Big Indian Slough in the southeast corner of Padilla Bay. We had a living crabapple blind that we sit under there on the slope of the dike and we had a couple of dozen of our hand carved teal and wigeon decoys out on the slough waters before us. The action was only so so with two or three teal in the bag. With little warning, the air over the rig was thick with wigeon and Tom got into action. He dropped two with his first round and gets a third with a second shot from his Uncle's 1921 16 ga. Model 12. That sort of thing makes any day special so as Tom picked and dressed our bag—on the spot—I told him just how special these days are, especially when he dresses the game. He agreed, and reminded me that at almost forty years his senior he doubts that I have the strength to do it. Good cronies are a precious thing!

Up until the time we sold the Shanty, Tom Newell and I made one "tradition-al" hunt each season. The rules were simple. We'd set our decoys in the Triangle marsh with the Shanty in view. We tried for a pair of birds, big, ducks, mallard or sprig, or one of each. When we bagged these, the decoys were picked up and the hunt was over for the day. Back at the Shanty, Tom picked and drew the birds as I built a fire in the wood stove and attended to a few other items on our never varied menu. It was sweet potatoes, canned peaches, fresh garlic bread (oven toasted), and roast duck. At the outset, of course, we'd each pour a belt of rye. During the baking of the fowl and sweet potatoes we generally grew somewhat mellow. Old tales were retold and embellished. New hunts were planned and new decoys designed. Alterations to our sneakboxes were also discussed as well as new ways to rig out. All was duck talk. There were no politics, crude jokes, family matters, or for that mat-ter, nothing that did not in some way associate with waterfowling. As a part of all this, Delphie had thrown out an old pair of wallabies of mine and rightly so as they were pretty raunchy. I took them over to the Shanty, painted a circle the size of a silver dollar on the toe of each—red on the left, and green on the right. Even after four belts I could still get my slippers on right. Almost always. The single day just described was our only day of serious imbibing throughout the season.

Jack Brewton, my long time friend and art agent, came up in the early eighties to hunt for a couple of days with Tom and me. Our plan was to hunt the Triangle marsh area not far from the Shanty. We decided to use the Gregor fourteen footer to trans-port Jack and Tom, and I ran my sneakbox also with some decoys. We started out in the dark from Tom Bergams landing up on the North Fork. Tom had designed a spray shield for his skiff to provide for a drier ride in rough seas. As we started down river this particular morning, Tom had seated Jack on the bow seat for the best trim. As we pulled away from the marina dock Tom opened the throttle of his fifteen Evinrude, and at once the boat was up on plane and scatting along about 25.

Tom had not tied the folded spray shield down and suddenly the wind created by the boat's speed blew the spray shield up and the stainless steel hoop that forms the shield's arc hit Jack in the back of the neck. The story goes that Jack was floored. I do know that when we all arrived at the blind down river and daylight was then at hand, my first impression of Jack was he looked a little starry-eyed. At a later time I found a white hard hat at a junk store and wrote "JACK" across the front in bold black letters. It still hangs in my gear shed awaiting Jack's return.

The three of us had a great time for two days. As I recall we had nearly thirty ducks at the finish. Tom also bagged his first snow goose on the last day. On one of the days, Jack waded out to pick up a bufflehead he'd downed. There was a bit of current in the marsh channel where we'd rigged and the duck was moving down channel. Not fast, but moving. Jack started out but failed to pull his left boot all the way up. Almost, but not quite. As he sloshed along trying to catch up with the duck we could see that the water was deepening as he moved along. The bird was almost at hand but the water was also nearing Jack's lowest boot tip. All the time Tom kept whispering, "pull up your boot, Jack." I wondered why Tom didn't shout this out so our guest could hear the warning. Very shortly it didn't matter—Jack was over his low boot. Tom promptly dubbed him Sir Low Boot Brewton.

Very late in Lady's life she would still accompany me when I used the sneakbox in the North Fork marsh. As I rowed about setting the decoys or gathering blinding material, the old girl enjoyed riding on the bow deck of the Barnegat. Her body, most ample by then, found this expanse just right—especially with two or three burlap decoy sacks spread out for padding.

One day, late in the season, we rigged for bluebills in a major channel that bisected the Triangle marsh close by the Shanty. I set a couple dozen Dunlap Bay model scaup blocks and blinded the boat close up against a wall of dense cattails. It was a fair day with light winds. One of those days that frequently induced dozing, unless the birds flew well. As the tide made and mid-morning came and passed, I began having some doubts about any duck movement at all. Sure, the faithful wintering buffleheads were about and dragged the rig repeatedly—some even landed. But I was set on some bluebills that day, so took no buffies.

As time dragged along, and the rising water crept up the cattail stems, a few birds did start to use the marsh. Mostly mallards coming in from open bay waters. There were a few wigeon and sprig, and, of course, those faithful greenwings. I still bit the bullet and held back in hopes of some scaup.

In time, my patience was rewarded and the bluebills moved. I took a drake or two as singles came to me. Lady was most pleased as I'd row out to pick them up. For, you see, by now I rowed out to make the retrieves. Rather, we did. As the sneakbox eased up to the duck, the old girl would lean over from her throne on the foredeck and gently pluck the bird from the water. Not exactly a picture that would gain attention if used as a "dramatic" scene for a dog chow ad, eh? But it suited our times, Lady and me, and after all, the birds were still brought to bag.

With little warning a really nice bundle of bluebills came around the point and into the channel. Low to the water, maybe twenty feet up, they bored on straight for the rig. I had time to get set and took a drake at about thirty yards, another as they tore by out about that same distance, and a third as the gang went dead away. The last drake was still swimming, head up and strong, so my favorite trap load came out to anchor him.

I've hunted ducks for sixty-eight years and triples have not dominated my shooting by any means. Those that I have pulled off were mostly on mallards as the bunch flared off over the decoys. The easiest kind of triple next to water sluicing, I have to admit. As the old gal and I rowed quietly about picking up the trio of bluebills, all seemed very right in the world. I knew Lady's string was fast running out, and this day would be more special for me as my years passed. Here we sat with five drake greater scaup carefully laid out on the foredeck so she could count and savor them. Did we need yet another bird to "limit out"? I felt not. The day had been perfect to this point. Leave it at that. We picked up and went home.

Early in January of the same year, the last day of the season, Lady and I went down to Fort Island in the Gregor to try for some goldeneye. I rigged only eight or ten decoys and anchored off to one side of the blocks. Lady was on the fore seat of the skiff on a foam pad. The day was calm and the bird flight almost nil. Lady lay on the padded seat with her muzzle over the gunnel. In time, three goldeneye came over the rig and I dropped one. We rowed out, I picked it up in a smelt net, handed it over for the old girl to retrieve. We called it a day and picked up. Lady passed on in the Spring.

CHAPTER 8

Padilla Bay

PADILLA BAY, TEN MILES NORTH OF LACONNER and accessible via the slough by boat offers somewhat different kinds of waterfowling than does the marshes of the Skagit River's deltas. This large bay hosts black brant, divers, sea ducks, and puddlers in great variety. There is no marsh habitat up on Padilla; just open water and several sand islands that offer limited shore hunting. It was the brant, of course, that captured my almost total interest back then, although today, as branting is becoming more and more restricted, the hunting of ducks takes on great importance.

On Padilla, most brant are taken from open water rigs. Floats are of most interest, as this contrivance is, to my knowledge, totally unique to this one bay. Not in my fifty-two years of hunting brant on every bay of our coast did I see anything used that even resembled a brant float.

Basically, it is a small house perched on a log raft. The rafts vary in size as do the houses. The largest rafts of logs can be 18 x 60 feet. Comprised of several large logs cabled and chained together, these rafts are awesome. The house on these larger models can accommodate up to five gunners. The floats differ mainly from the boats used for brant hunting in that they are rafts and can be moved only by towing whereas boats have their own power.

A brant float is anchored in the bay a few days before the season opens, and is left in place for the duration of that season. Only rarely are floats moved to new locations during the season. Some are torn loose from their anchorings during violent storms and then, of course, find new locations—locations so remote they are never seen again! Decoys are the single most important part of a brant rig on the bay—be it a float or a boat. Decoys are now and were in the past a combination of silhouette (shadow) clusters on boards as well as full bodied decoys. Today few hand made full bodied decoys are to be seen, with the exception of my own rig and possibly a few others. Plastic decoys are the norm. Hand made decoys, so common years ago, are now all in private collections.

Mit Harlan of Dunlap Towing writes: "Since Dunlap Towing Company has no

A LARGE FLOAT WITH BOAT SLIP

A MIDGET WITH BARRELS FOR FLOATION

A MEDIUM SIZED FLOAT WITH FLOATING SHADOWS STOWED ABOARD

LARGE FLOAT, ARTFULLY CAMOUFLAGED - BOAT SLIP & CAR TIRES AS BUMPERS

MEDIUM SIZE - WOOD STOVE - LOCKABLE DECOY STORAGE - TANKS OR FOAM BILLETS FOR FLOATATION - AGAIN SOME ATTEMPT AT CAMOUFLAGE

A SMALL SPARTAN FLOAT - LOG - FLOATS - WOODEN LADDER.

I TOURED THE BAY AFTER THE SEASON HAD CLOSED AND MADE PHOTOS OF THIS COLLECTION OF FLOATS. THE YEAR 1984

David Hagenbaumer

recorded history of hunting exploits, facts sometimes become somewhat muddled. However, it is certain that the floats used to brant hunt are the product of combining a working tool with the ingenuity of tug boaters and hunters.

"Beginning in the late 1940's and continuing until 1996, Dunlap leased a large tract of tideland on the west side of Padilla Bay known as the Whitmarsh log storage. This storage was used for storing Hemlock pulp logs, some of which were so heavy that they sank or became deadheads. To move these heavy logs from the storage area to the mill, "mats" were made by lashing boomsticks to a couple of cross logs forming a floating platform which the deadheads were put onto and then towed. The men that worked in the log storages were, almost to a man, waterfowl hunters as were their customers. It was only natural that as they worked around the brant in Padilla Bay, they began to shoot more and more of these fine tasting birds.

"The first Dunlap Brant hunting blind in Padilla bay was a dolphin driven north of the log storage. Birds were also hunted from the anchored tugboat. However, Manfred Nystrom is credited with revolutionizing the Brant hunting from Dunlap's perspective by using the deadhead mats as floating blinds. When the mats were first used, the hunters would lie on the boomsticks behind the log that was lashed behind them. With a large spread of silhouettes and blocks, this proved to be an effective way to hunt Brant.

"To improve the hunter's comfort as well as to mask the movement of the impatient, Manfred built what some of his contemporaries referred to as a pig house on the float. This was a low, three-sided shed with a fence about three feet in the front of the open side which hid the occupants from view of the approaching birds. The addition of the shed, with charcoal heating and seating did not seem detrimental to the hunting, or at least not enough to give up these creature comforts.

"Over the years since we first used floats, the dolphin has been abandoned, the tower that was north of the sand islands is no longer used, and we no longer hunt on the west side of the Swinomish Channel, but we still use two floats, each anchored with two large danforth anchors to hunt brant on the east side of the channel. Because of the severity of the weather, and the velocity of the tidal current, we believe that the only practical ways to hunt brant in Padilla Bay are either from a float or a boat. We feel the floats are safer, more comfortable and usually just as productive."

When boats are used to hunt brant on Padilla Bay they had best be craft of great seaworthiness as the shallow waters of Padilla can become violent on very short notice. Just this past season, Worth Mathewson and I had been invited to hunt from the Dunlap Float on opening day. When we arrived at the Wannigan at the break of day, a north wind had come up. Although the young men had been able to set the decoys around the float, in the brief interval of less than an hour the seas had built up on the open bay to such proportions that disembarking from Dunlap's twenty-two foot Woolridge work boat onto the float deck was too dangerous. Mit Harlan, whose responsibility it was to make the judgment call said simply "it's a no go." So, we spent a pleasant morning in the Wannigan in front of the wood stove, hoping the wind might go down. Periodically, the boat handlers that day, who were Mike Harlan and Kenny Hanson, would sally forth to check the open bay conditions. It stayed a no go until noon when we finally left to do some duck hunting down south in the north fork marsh. This drill is not at all uncommon for the brant hunters of Padilla Bay.

A few miles north, eight maybe, is Samish Island. From the western end of the island, a gravel spit juts out in a southerly direction into the shallows that surround

the island. This gravel spit has long been a favored gravelling spot for the sea geese as well as a favored hunting location for the Samish Island Brant Club.

I've had the opportunity to be the guest of Dr. Morrie Johnson at this club on three occasions. Once I had sat in the blind and bagged a brant. On the most recent visit I was content to sit in the clubhouse drinking coffee and watching the others through the large picture window as they shared the blind in shifts. They bagged ten birds during the day. Worth Mathewson was also a guest on this day and got his two bird limit shortly after lunch time.

Both the Padilla brant floats, Dunlap Towing Company's in particular, and the Samish Island Brant Club, are historic fixtures in this area. Fixtures, I fear, that have a doubtful life span if the past brant season of five days is any indicator of the future of branting in Washington. I mean this as no criticism of those who regulate our wildfowl. If these highly restrictive seasons will benefit a given species then I am in favor of curtailment, or closure if necessary. In fact, the season on brant was closed in Washington during the years of 1983 through 1986 in order to see if more brant would winter on the bays rather than going to Mexico.

Samish Bay borders Padilla Bay on the north. Here, brant hunting is done primarily from stake or stilt blinds much like those so common on many of the bays and sounds of the East Coast, and on Humbolt Bay in Northern California as well as Tomales a bit further south in California. A few branters also gun from boats as they do on Padilla. However, no floats, as described earlier, are used.

A couple of seasons back, Jerry Lomesdalen of Bow, Washington, invited me to be a guest gunner on one of his two stake blinds. I shared this four person blind with an old friend, Bryce Barden, of Burlington, Washington. Bryce took his own work skiff for transport to the blind and to carry forty of the hand carved decoys of several carvers (mine included). This was a special hunt for me—a first from a Pacific Coast stake blind. Well, actually, my second, as years ago, circa 1960, I sneaked onto a stake blind in Humboldt Bay that I found unattended with the blessings of some dockside gents that assured me that the owner wouldn't mind. I shot no brant that day as it turned out. Perhaps the owner of the blind had placed a hex on any trespassers! But, back to Samish Bay.

In the predawn darkness, Bryce piloted his skiff away from the launch on the Samish River following Jerry driving his twenty foot work boat. It was well that we had Jerry ahead as he knows that tortuous river channel like the back of his hand. Slender willow wands mark the channel proper but in the darkness they are all but invisible. Eventually, we reached the bay proper and only then felt the full thrust of the stiff wind we'd live with until mid afternoon. Jerry guided us to the stake blind we would use that day and we proceeded to set our decoys. One of Jerry's hands took Bryce's skiff back to the other blind where it would remain all day being used as a retriever boat when brant were downed by gunners of either blind. Jerry's larger boat was anchored a ways off, but Bryce's skiff was tied up to the second blind. In essence, we were marooned out there on the blind we were in. Nothing to fret over, of course, as we were in radio communication all day with the blind a half

mile away where both boats were anchored—no different from many hunts I've made on the East Coast on several of the bays and sounds where stake blinds were used a good many years ago. I'll wager that many are used still in spite of much reduced bag limits on that coast.

This day on Samish dawned wet, dreary, and blustery. The wind was a typical winter southerly. The rain typically heavy at times. The combination of wet and blustery made it dreary. Some of the hand carved brant decoys were prototypes I'd made only a few days prior to this hunt. Actually, I was pleased to see rough sea conditions that would be the perfect field test for my new prototypes of several styles. The rest of my personal rig consisted of decoys by famous west coast carvers such as Pinches, Saylor, Newell, Columbia River Decoys and my own, some of which were made thirty years before. These decoys needed no testing. They had seen the drill on many a bay, some since the late fifties.

Few birds flew that day and as I recall, Bryce bagged one and Dr. Donald Boettner, the third member of our blind, also brought one to hand. Jerry had asked us not to shoot any ducks as there were plenty about and had we shot all those that provided us with an opportunity to do so, the pick-up boat would have been shuttling back and forth ceaselessly. I did violate Jerry's rule, however, and shot a perfect drake greater scaup for a reference specimen. Jerry was most gracious over this and made no fuss.

During the course of this day, the radio crackled to let us know that Federal wardens had just checked the home blind and that the officers were headed our way. They arrived shortly, and with some difficulty one officer managed to get from the heaving boat onto the ladder of the blind. He clung to the top of the blind while standing on the top rung of the ladder. He checked our licenses, guns and shells. I felt sort of guilty that no one invited him aboard. It seemed a tad inhospitable to me, but then I was just a guest myself and felt no need to play host. We got a clean bill of health and the other officer who had stood off in the rough seas came into the wind and gingerly plucked the officer on the ladder aboard the heaving whaler.

While the day was only fair as so far as brant went, it was a smash in other ways. Just to be out there in a stake blind, miles from solid ground is always a strange and special feeling. A thrill, in fact. The sea/bay life one encounters out there in open water is a constant parade of species. Mammals and birds. Many harbor seals paraded past the decoys and ducks of several species decoyed readily. Scaup, bufflehead, scoters, and goldeneyes came into the decoys all day. Sprig, mal-

lards, wigeon, and a few teal passed us by en route from the mainland to Samish Island and visa versa. They had no intention of landing in the decoys, but often flew low over the rig. One little bluebill hen spent an hour or two in and about the decoys diving and feeding merrily away. For the bird watchers a day aboard a stake blind would be a treat like few others. For photographers, such a day would provide picture opportunities galore. In fact, a vast majority of my personal collection of reference photos of waterfowl flight were made by my using a Nikon motor drive—1959 vintage—from a blind and over decoys. Exactly as I would hunt these birds—substituting gun for camera being the sole difference.

With the tide well out by now, Jerry made the call to wind it up. The decoy skiff arrived and we quickly hauled the lot aboard on the long lines. I instructed the young haulees to not bother with anchors and line wrapping. The weather by now had worsened and in my judgment time was of the essence. Much better to untangle the mess next day in the warmth of my gear shed rather than get thumped around out there on the lumpy bay waters any longer than absolutely necessary.

Again, with darkness at hand we followed Jerry back into the river and close on his transom threaded our way back through the channel's windings and up to the moorage. A perfect day indeed. As Heilner would most likely have said, "I'll take a stake blind every time."

The stake blind we used that day was built by Jerry in 1985. It is shown here in the story. Here, I might add that what I call stake blinds, or stilt blinds, are generally referred to as "stands" by the men who build and shoot from them here on Samish Bay. After years of damage by ice and gale force winds that cost Jerry three stands, he designed a new concept—one that still stands today. Instead of pilings or dimension lumber to serve as the stand's legs or supporting members, his present blind has four inch angle iron as legs. I was surprised when he told me that these iron legs are not driven into the bay bottom as the other stands out there. Jerry rather, has affixed more angle irons to the bottom of the legs so that these lie on the bottom and form a twenty-four foot platform. This creates a very stable unit under reasonable weather conditions but in gale or ice conditions will allow the stand to tip over helping to prevent total loss. No, no one has been in one of Jerry's stands when it tipped over. Mr. Lomesdalen is far too skilled a waterman to risk his guest's lives in days of such weather. All stay ashore.

On brant days with moderate weather, I would launch my sneakbox under the Highway 20 bridge and run north up channel. When a bit past the last sand island, I'd cut out to the east and into the bay proper. When about a quarter of a mile into the main bay, I'd rig about two dozen to thirty full bodied decoys. Sometimes on single anchors but more frequently on long lines holding eight decoys each. The ground lines are ¾₆ inch halibut line and each decoy has a 12 inch length of electrical wire attached. This is solid #12 copper wire insulated in black plastic. At the other end of this wire is a halibut snap. The main line is anchored with concrete anchors cast in one gallon milk jugs. Eye bolts are set in each anchor for bronze snap attachment with the main line. These anchors weigh about ten pounds each. Anchors, any lighter, sometimes drag when there is a lot of floating eelgrass that collects on the decoys and the main line between lead decoy and on down to the anchor. At times, even these concrete anchors cannot hold the mass of eelgrass that collects. Once I have three lines of decoys set, the boat gets it's covering of shrimp net and is anchored to a single line parallel to the decoy strings and twenty yards away from the middle string. This boat anchor line need be, in our water depth of 12 to 15 feet, about 75 feet long. I use a 15 pound danforth anchor at each end. In the middle of the line I tie a crab bouy painted black and white. To this bouy I snap on a short line from the sneakbox bow handle. Twelve feet from the bouy I snap to the main line, a three foot line attached to the stern handle of the sneakbox. Unsnapping to retrieve birds and then returning to hook up again is very simple. I used to use a single bow anchor but frequently found the boat doing too much "wandering" during conflicts with changing currents and winds.

With the boat anchored and decoys rigged, I lie down in the sneakbox on a pad of closed cell foam. I have a piece of plywood 18 x 24 inches that I prop against the

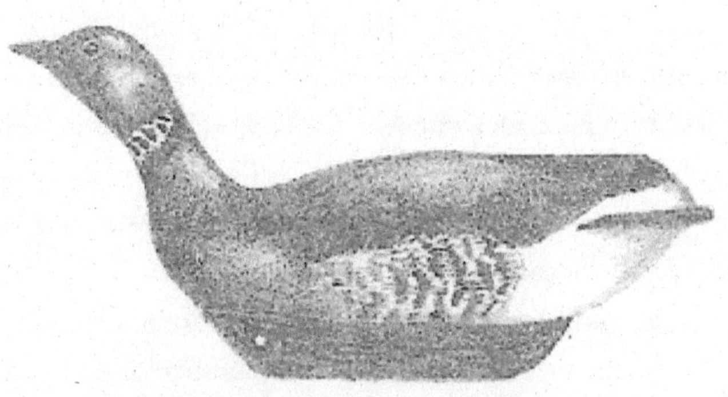

PAT O'HAGAN - ARLINGTON
CIRCA 1995 - HOLLOW CEDAR

MANFRED NYSTROM
LA CONNER - CIRCA 1940

DAVE HAGERBAUMER - BURLINGTON
1995 - HOLLOW RED CEDAR

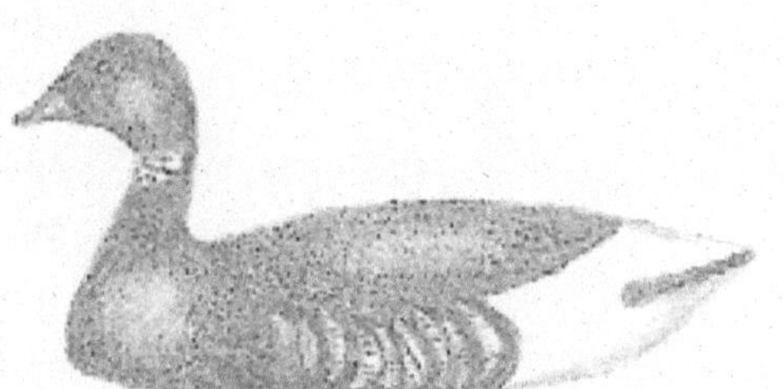

TOM NEWELL - GIG HARBOR
CIRCA 1995 - HOLLOW CEDAR

DAVE HAGERBAUMER - 1984
HIGH DENSITY BALSA

DAVE HAGERBAUMER
1995 - HIGH DENSITY BALSA

fore deck at a slant with the bottom resting on the foam pad. I lay back against this back rest with my head no higher above the deck than the outboard on the transom. I cover the outboard, by the way, with the same shrimp net that covers the boat itself. My sneakbox has a couple of dozen oar lock seats scattered about on the gunnels, boat deck, and transom. The seats have sockets a half inch in diameter. My confidence gull decoys also have 1 inch dowel stakes so these can be arranged over the boat as I choose. It's a darn slick one-man sans dog rig. About as deadly a rig, but not quite as deadly as a sink box. The sneakbox, as fine a sea boat as it is, has limitations with regard to rough weather. The operator of these boats must be the sole judge of what the boat can or cannot do—safely.

Along the west side of Padilla bay there runs a navigational channel. It is bouyed and dolphined with channel markers, lights and numbers. I do not know it's mean low water depth, but it does handle large fishing boats, sailboats and yachts. When this channel was established years back, the Corps of Engineers pumped the dredging spoil on the west side of the new channel. This spoil, mostly sand, formed three good sized "islands." All are only slightly higher than the highest tides, so have a ring around their tops of logs, and other flotsam indigenous to any tidal bay. I have no idea as to the ownership of these islands. Some say the state owns them and some insist they are privately owned. I do know that they provide, at times, fine duck and brant hunting from their shores. While I've tried this, several times I much prefer to hunt the small bay behind the islands, with my sneakbox as a layout boat. I've had many fine days here with brant, scaup, and wigeon. And now and then a mallard or sprig, although these not so trusting species find the netted over Barnegat hard to swallow. On very tempestuous days fair mallard and pintail gunning can be had, but don't count on it on fair days.

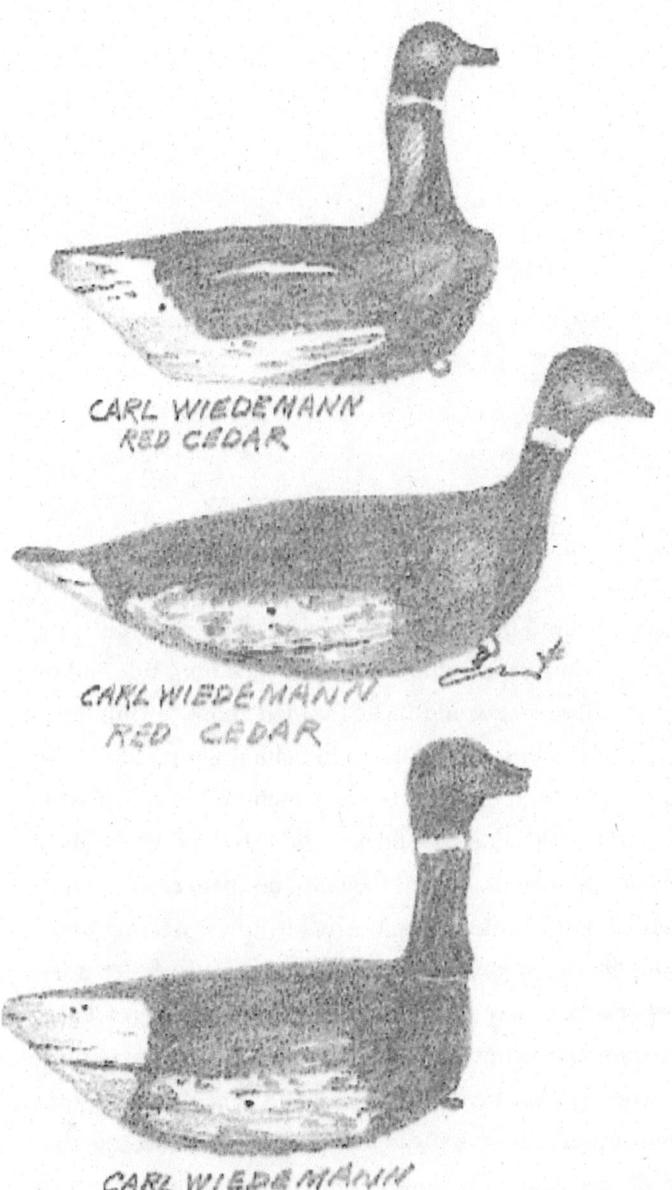

CARL WIEDEMANN
RED CEDAR

CARL WIEDEMANN
RED CEDAR

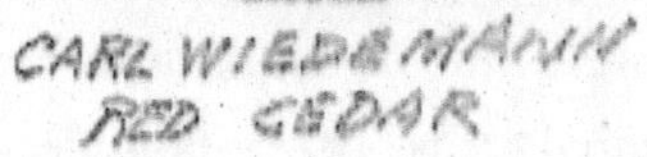

CARL WIEDEMANN
RED CEDAR

PHIL ESARY
RED CEDAR

HANK AND MIKE PLOEG
RED CEDAR

HANK AND MIKE PLOEG
RED CEDAR

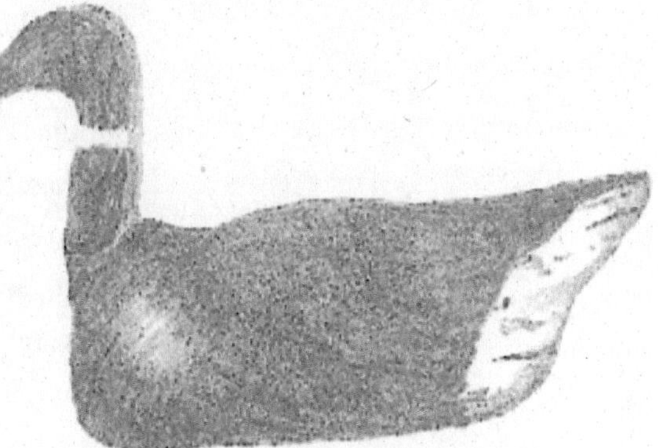

HANK AND MIKE PLOEG
RED CEDAR

BRANT DECOYS OF SAMISH BAY

CHAPTER 9

Close To Home

TWO SEASONS BACK I MADE A BRANT HUNT on the last day of the season in the waters behind the largest Sand Island. I stuck to my usual routine on this day and came into the bay on the incoming tide and on the lowest water in which the Barnegat would float. I waded about setting thirty decoys on individual lines. There is little tidal current in behind the islands so the decoys were rigged in a loose "pod" and the sneakbox was anchored on the up wind edge of this grouping. This day I also added confidence gulls to the decks as these birds are very common around the islands. In fact, they nest on them each summer. With all in readiness, I settled down in the cockpit. Already, it was nearing noon. (One hunts on tidal bays by the tide book, not the clock or sun.) I had seen a few bundles of brant out over the main bay heading south toward their gravelling beaches. Some scaup were coming into my little bay and now and then one or more were tempting shots but my goal was brant first and ducks second. Some time passed, an hour, a half hour, I don't know, but suddenly here they came, low over the water around the end of the island. There were nine or ten birds in the flock and at once spotted my rig from a couple of hundred yards out. As if on a leash, the group homed right on in. They dropped their gear and set their wings and at forty yards I met them head on.

The first bird dropped stone cold at about thirty-five yards and the second, three heart beats later. He showed some signs of life so I shot him over again. I carry number six steel for this job. The survivors swung wide and landed up bay not more than three hundred yards from me. At times brant can be deceptively trusting, and at other times exasperatingly wary. Only one of the reasons I guess, that the species holds my favoritism, and has since I bagged my first one in 1946. So here I sit with a limit of branta nigricans. Lots of time before the tide starts back out so why not some scaup? Lots of fowl movement now—ducks and brant. Brant in twos and threes and small bundles keep decoying but it is duck I can shoot now. Often there are brant swimming in the decoys, only to flush as I rise to kill or miss a bluebill or wigeon. Another hour passes and now it is all over. A mixed limit of

Shown here is blind number one of the Samish Bay Sports Club, Inc. It is located near the Eastern end of the club's marsh and perches at the tip of a grassy spit. This blind is one I favored during the year I held my "gunning" membership. This is the blind from which Tom Albrect (one of the four original members) and I shot, one very stormy day, two limits of teal and wigeon. While I do not know Tom's score, I still smart in recalling that I burned up nineteen shells to bag six ducks. My feeble excuse was the wind! I depict here one of the club's staple duck species —— elegant green-wings.

A couple of seasons ago my friend, Steve Wohlwend, a shareholder in the Samish Bay Sports Club, Inc. invited me to share his blind with him and his Illinois croney of many years, Terry Cross. The brant flew well as did the ducks. I shot poorly, which is not unusual, but as always had a great time. The view here is from our blind — looking East toward the Cascades with the Chuckanut Hills in the foreground.

A fine day with the sprig at the Samish Bay Sports Club. This day, circa 1980, I was rigged with mallards but the pintails simply would not leave me alone! Tough way to make a living, eh?

bluebills and wigeon and two brant. It has been yet another text book three hours there in the little bay behind the Middle Sand Island. If my old bones don't creak too much next season, I believe I'll give it another go. In preparation for the nine-ty-five-ninety-six fowling season, I worked several hours the summer before, redesigning my sneakbox netting blind to accommodate me in sitting up position, as on a chair. In prior years, I sat up on a boat cushion with my legs extended flat out on the cockpit floor. I began to find this very tiring and to get to my feet quick-ly has become impossible. I am now seventy-seven years old and things simply do not work right anymore. Delphie gave me a cap for my birthday this year which reads: "THIS IS WHAT OLD LOOKS LIKE". With my newly designed net blind I can sit on my shooting box with two boat cushions atop and have my legs in a comfortable position that allows me to stand to shoot. This new blind adds more profile to the boat but by setting up adjacent to willows, cattails, or other tall growth, the birds seem not to notice it at all.

In preparation for the 95/96 season I set a number of three as a personal bag limit on ducks—all to be drakes when identification was possible. I'm not on any crusade, mind you, I've certainly limited out a big plenty since I shot my first duck in 1929. Three ducks are a big plenty for Delphie and me. It also is a good feeling to know I can still practice some control. On the last day of the season in early January 1996 I set up on Otter Point in the north fork marsh. This point is formed where two large tidal guts merge and create a body of water about a hundred yards wide. A nice expanse where decoys show up like a wart on the nose—even at low tide. In addition, there is a healthy stand of cattails close to a mooring point where my new higher profile boat blind can blend in beautifully.

The incoming tide started around 1100 hours and I was there by noon to rig out. By 1300 all was ready and I settled back on my throne of boat cushions atop the shooting box. No flight really started until an hour or more later, but when it did, the ducks and I went at it hot and heavy. In short order, I had three greenheads on the fore deck and was actually standing up unloading my elderly L.C. Smith with rabbit ears when along comes a drake can! He drug the rig and peeled off to his port and by jingo came around again! I was loaded up in plenty of time to meet him head on and the day was mine in a blaze of glory! What a season's end. I plead guilty to exceeding my personal limit, but this bull was only the second one I've seen in the north fork marsh in almost twenty years. Besides, the Devil made me do it. Bless his little black heart.

I learned how good the Dungeness variety of crabs were way back during my Ashland years when Louie Gephart brought them over from Humboldt Bay on his frequent visits to hunt and see Shakespearean plays. Since those initial tastings, I've been a crab addict. Frozen or canned crab are junk food as far as I'm concerned, so catching, cooking and eating on the same day has been my M.O. since then. Up here in Puget Sound, crabbing opportunities are plentiful and over the course of the nearly twenty years that Delphie and I have lived here, we have sorted out a couple of places that we favor—one in Padilla bay and one in Skagit Bay. On a pleasant summer day we enjoy using rings that catch crabs much faster than a crab trap. (locally called "pots") The rings must be constantly tended and re-baited as necessary. If not, the bait is consumed and the crabs simply walk away. Baited pots on the other hand lure crabs into their confines through two tunnels with triggers that prevent escape. Small crabs are able to escape at will through openings in the pot walls that are just small enough to prevent legal sized crabs from getting out. We use rings in the summer for a fun time outing, but I set pots during the winter months when being on the water is mostly a not so pleasant time weather-wise. Pots need to be left out about 72 hours to do a good job. A longer time serves little purpose as the bait sours and lures few or no more crabs. Should bad weather prevent running the pots for a longer period of time, no harm is done as the legal crabs cannot escape and certainly will not starve.

Many years ago I saw an older fellow several times crabbing commercially with rings. This was on Alsea Bay in Oregon during the wintertime. His boat was a wooden 25 footer rigged with a hand operated davit and block. He set about 15 rings always in the channel of the bay that was closest to the "jaws" or entrance to

PROTOTYPE - When I lived in Oregon I designed this decoy for use on Coos Bay, my favorite commercial area. Before I got around to carving the rig I moved north. This prototype was hollow red cedar with a sugar pine head.

the ocean proper. He set the baited rings in a line that followed the deeper waters of this channel—about 20 feet. Once set, he would return to the first ring set, remove legal crabs, re-bait and go to the next ring. Once at the end of the "string" enough time had elapsed to start all over again. When crabs are plentiful, 20 minutes is time enough to lure plenty onto the bait. After watching this old gent on several occasions I had the opportunity to meet him when we both arrived at the McKinley marina at the same time. I was hauling my skiff out as he was mooring his at a berth he kept year around. We struck up a conversation and I learned that he was a retired commercial fisherman who could no longer endure the rigors of that demanding occupation but neither could he endure leaving the trade entirely. He explained that the overhead with his small boat and gear was minimal. He did not have to meet larger vessel payments, fuel costs were small, no crew shared his profit, and he could fish (crab) when he chose. That day his wooden fish box held almost one hundred and fifty pounds of dungeness crab. These were great crabs, many seven inches, a size commonly called "ocean crabs". Crab prices vary greatly from year to year depending on a variety of factors. Crab populations, supplies held over, and so forth. But even on a low price cycle this old gent still had a hundred to a hundred and fifty dollars worth of Dungeness there in his fish box! I think of that elderly man now and again even to this day. It was so very obvious that he was doing exactly what he loved. Never will I pull a crab ring without thinking of him—and so it goes.

Along a highway that leads east out of the Skagit Valley is a small and narrow lake, surrounded by cottonwood, fir and willow. Throughout it has emergent growth of several native grasses. Here and there are little patches of open water. Main, it is used by teal, woodducks, and mallards. Ring necked ducks are the most common divers. I was not aware that this lake even existed until one day a young man called to ask if I would do a painting for him depicting a special day he had experienced some time earlier when he bagged some redheads on the lake. The lake has no launch for boats and any easy access is across private land. The day Jeff took me to the lake to gather reference for the painting we had to climb down a steep bank through wild blackberries to reach the water. Once I gathered the photo and field sketch reference material needed to finish the painting I could not get this little lake out of my mind. It followed, of course, that I went back one season to hunt. I chose an area that Jeff showed me where one could wade to set decoys and retrieve as by now, Lady had passed on. On a week day that storm winds had been forecasted for the Straits, and 40 knots plus for the valley, the lake beckoned. I felt that those sheltered waters would be black with fowl. Knowing that at my age, just getting down the slope to the lake would be a challenge, not to mention the climb out, a very spare outfit was an absolute necessity. I made up a kit that included a nice 870 in 28 ga. with 26"IMP. CYL. BBL., six balsa life size teal decoys and two balsa mallard, one timber call by Iverson and 10 shells with no. six lead shot. This was three or so years before steel came in.

I was fighting my way down the bank through the undergrowth at first good

To protect farmlands from tidal flooding a dike encircles the South end of Padilla bay. Shown here at low tide is a very old boat house alongside the dike on the mud flats of Big Indian Slough. A nearby hunting club uses this old boat house to store decoys and gunning boats. Now and then I gun for teal over decoys on this slough. David Hagerbaumer 1998

light. While the water was not "black with fowl" as I broke through the growth at the shore of the lake, several mallards did flush close in, with the hens squawking their heads off—their calling echoing up and down the lake. I was pleased to jump the mallards as this suggested that no one else was on the lake. And being a week day I hadn't really expected to encounter anyone else. After wading out in knee deep water to rig my meager spread of decoys in an open spot in the grass, I made no effort to build any sort of blind. Just sat down on the bank of the lake under the drooping branches of a large fir. I was completely hidden from above and by sitting still no decoying birds would ever spot me in the shadow of the fir tree. As best as I could judge it, I sat about 20 or so yards from the decoys. While setting the decoys, a few teal flitted about and a small bundle of mallards started to decoy but flared out and went on down lake. I feel it was the same bunch that got up when I first came in. Barely settled, a lone shot rang out from the far end of the lake—maybe

five hundred yards off. I had no idea who shot what, but shortly a half dozen teal, fifty yards out, spotted my eight decoys and wheeled in.

They landed before I could even get into action but on the rise I downed one stone cold. There is no current in this lake, and on this day the light wind in these protected waters would not move my bird, so I sat tight. Smart move, as in the space of a couple of minutes three woodies came about in a half circle and set their wings. I got one on my second shot, but the overhanging limb got in the way of a third. To take care of this problem I just moved out a few feet from under the limb. Still no need to build a blind. Two birds, three shots. Good. It's gonna be some morning! A lull set in and for a half an hour or more not a feather was to be seen. Com'on, I still have seven shells left and this day is barely started. As the morning brightened through the high overcast of racing clouds, a bunch of birds did move over high in the direction of the river a half mile to the south. In short order, more went over, two or three, small bunches, and even bundles of thirty or more. Still though, no action on the lake. Directly, I started to hear distant shooting from the direction of the river. Likely, I thought, some fellas who'd gone to the considerable effort to rig a big bunch of decoys in slack water at the foot of a river bar. These are common all along the lower Skagit. Not long after the shooting over the river a bunch of five or six mallards came over the trees on the edge of the lake across from me. I gave them a greeting call to get their attention and, by jingo, they curled around and came right at my rig. They must'a just had a going over on the river because they went on down lake and out of sight. In moments they returned coming toward me. This time they knew there were friends on the water in front of the old fir. I gave only the feed call, and again they showed interest. Around they went in a wide circle only to come back at a hail call. As mallards are in the habit of doing, this circling went on for a bit. I'd call a little at the outside of each circle and then chuckle as they came at me. Finally, at the far side of one circle, some one duck in that flight made the decision and in they came. Feet down and committed.

I shot three times to put two birds down and one was only winged. I got another shell into the 870 in time to anchor the crip with the load. Now, this is more like it! As I fed my last three shells into the little Remington, I made a pact with myself that I'd shoot no more than twice at any more ducks just in case that last shell was needed for another cripple. A bit more time passed before a great lot of teal engulfed my end of the lake. I mean a lot of teal! Fifty or more birds—just like a swarm of bumble bees they came, as only teal can—all at once. Some were on the water before I could move, others were wheeling about trying to figure out just what they were going to do with all that unbridled energy. Very quickly I helped them decide and took a whack at a half dozen that came over the blocks. I missed one and then took one and that's all she wrote. I gathered my five birds, my decoys, and with one twenty-eight gauge shell left in my pocket, started to claw my way uphill through the brush. I've not gone back to the lake since. Not because I'm fearful of spoiling that first hunt with an inferior second but I'm doubtful these years later if I could handle that brushy slope again!

A lot of fellas hunt the drainage ditches in this vast agricultural valley named the Skagit. Just how many acres are in farmland I do not know, but I'll wager thousands. All are on the same level and are all drained by ditches that carry rain water back to the sea. Some ditches are small, one can step across them; others large, a hundred feet or more. Fowl of all species, other than sea ducks use these drainage ditches. Mostly, though, it's a mallard, teal and bufflehead show. They find some amount of food in these drains but I feel it is mostly a place to rest, especially on big storm days when the bays are a frothy mess.

I have friends up here that started to jump shoot ducks on these farm field drainages when they were in school in LaConner, and to this day, they still do it. Old habits are hard to break, I guess, and in this case it is a habit they're not likely to give up so long as they can walk. Being an inveterate decoy hunter, jump shooting was never a form of waterfowling I took at all seriously, so once I moved to the Skagit Valley it never occurred to me to take it up. I may have been missing something really good all these years but it's too late to start now as I'd have trouble walking far enough to make a meaningful ditch hunt anyway.

Early on, 1980 or 1981, I met a young fella by the name of Bryce Barden. He owned a sporting goods store in nearby Mount Vernon and right off we became friends. Bryce loves

One day I got tired of fighting the tides and the idea came to me to set up on Middle Sand Island at extreme high tide mark. I scratched out a nest in some grass amongst a lot of drift. My shadows were scattered about on the sandy knoll within thirty yards of the channel. I was set up by good light and then spent most of the day watching lots of brant who weren't the least bit interested in my new theory. I relaxed my vigil and you guessed it right there, a lone bird blundered by in range and caught me flat footed. No way to get switched around, so I slapped the old 870 to my port side and by jingus, I got that smart-aleck!

to hunt, salmon fish, and crab. One winter he asked me to go with him on a brant hunt off the mouth of Joe Leary Slough. This slough empties into Padilla Bay on the east shore near the bay's northerly end. Brant and divers like this area. We went in Bryce's boat and launched at Bayview public ramp. Bryce had a brand new Ithaca 10 ga. auto loader. In fact, I believe this was the gun's maiden voyage. We rigged some brant and bluebill decoys a couple of hundred feet off the mouth of the Slough, and netted the boat. Not once during that morning tide did any brant venture near us, but divers did and we had good shooting. Most were greater scaup.

At one point, Bryce asked me to try his ten gauge and handed me this cannon. In due course, what I reckoned was a hen bluebill came along right over the rig. I whaled away, and blamed if she didn't fold up! Upon retrieval, I was most surprised to see the bird was a hen redhead. When we got back to the launch, a Federal and a State warden greeted us. That was only the second time I have been checked in my eighteen years here in Puget Sound. When they checked our bag, one of the officers told me that my redhead was the only one he'd seen in a bag all season. I knew they were not numerous here on the coast so this bird made a sort of special day of it—that and the one shot I made with that three and half inch tank gun.

One time I went out with Bryce when he was still ring fishing commercially for dungeness crab. We fished Samish Bay that day with ten rings. Bryce ran the

rings, handed me the line which I threw around a wind-lass on a six horse Honda. The rings came aboard at a great speed. It was so slick and I was so impressed that I almost went out and bought an outfit for my eighteen foot work skiff. On second thoughts I decided the exercise was better for me in the long run. As I remember, we caught a couple of hundred pounds of crab that day. I know that Bryce sent me home with a pail full. On the way back we passed several stake blinds in the south end of the bay. These I photographed and have used as reference for my drawings in this book.

On the South Fork of the Skagit is some habitat much different from the more common tidal marsh of short grass and cattail. When the river rises, it floods an area of cottonwoods and alder trees that at first glance resembles closely the "green timber" of Arkansas. There is a spartan boat launch on the South Fork at the town of Conway. From this launch I made a number of forays downstream. Most led me to the foreshore marsh, identical in character to that of the North Fork, except down on the South Fork are most of the snow geese that winter on Skagit Bay. Biologists tell me that the reason is a simple one. The food most favored by our wintering snow geese, a tuber of three square grass, is found principally around the South Fork area. My trips via sneakbox to this marsh were for both snow geese and ducks. Geese have never held much interest for me but they did add some variety to duck hunting. My method for a snow goose/duck hunting combo was no different from the layout with sneakbox for ducks alone, except I added some snow goose decoys to the duck rig.

From time to time, Delphie would express interest in the goings on of this "hunting game." So I suggested that she be my non-shooting guest on a snow goose hunt on the foreshore of Skagit Bay off Fire Island. Her personal narration of that hunt follows:

"The Indians call them Wavys. I first thought it was because of the undulating motion of the wings but it isn't that at all. The Indian name for wild goose is Wa Wa, which through corruption has become wavy. So said Dave, as we sat warming ourselves before the fireplace and sipping a drink while talking over the day's hunt.

"It was the 2nd day in November and I had awakened this day anticipating my first waterfowl hunt with Dave. It was to be the "full route", as he put it. Being city raised and completely foreign to this type of activity made it something new and a very interesting experience for me. The hunting was to be done from a scull boat,

the entourage of decoys in tow via row boat. Dave's plan was to pole the boats out the channel on the incoming tide to the point he had picked to set up. The spot was on the foreshore between the south and north fork of the Skagit River. Lady, Dave's golden retriever and I were to walk across the marsh to meet him. Lady became quite anxious when she saw her beloved master poling down the channel without her. I convinced her she should stay with me and we took off across the marsh. She kept her eyes on Dave in the channel and made tracks for the meeting place while I stumbled along in oversize hip boots through muddy potholes and tall weeds in an effort to keep up with her.

"Although the rest of the hunt was spent on this same spot, it was an ever changing scene. The decoys were placed by Dave and my part was to unwrap the cord around each one and let each anchor lie free on the marsh. When the row boat was hidden behind a large tree stump, and the scull boat covered completely with netting and grass, we climbed aboard.

"This was time for pulling the cork on a hot thermos of coffee and the munching on a candy bar. By the time we were done the scene had changed. The four dozen or more decoys around us were now floating free. They were life-like in their various positions, bobbing and twisting with the movement of the tide. As I looked around, I thought to myself, this is like ACT I, SCENE II. The background music was the call of the gulls. In the distance, the movement of hundreds of snow geese flecked the sky in what appeared to be white confetti being blown in the wind. I could only liken the sound to that of hundreds of barking dogs. There was no other sign of life except for occasional birds coming in close.

"For each approach I asked the same question, 'what is it?' The answer was very patient, but always the same—' a gull' or `shore birds'. We became lulled into this pattern when suddenly the next answer, 'a gull' was quickly accompanied with 'heck, that's no gull, it's a snow goose!' Before the word 'goose' had completely formed on his lips, I heard a shot and saw the goose fall into the water. Instantly, Lady was over the side with encouraging words from Dave. 'Go get it, Lady.' It all happened within seconds—I needed more eyes to see everything. I watched Lady gently and tenderly bring the downed bird to the boat.

"A lull in any movement activity allowed time to again observe the changes that had taken place around us. What had been salt grass and pot holes before us was now a sea of gray water as far as the eye could see. A few sprinkles started, but with hip boots, rain pants, and rain jacket with hood, it was rather pleasant. This could be SCENE III, I thought. The only sound was that of the water lapping against the side of the boat, when suddenly the distant wild cries became louder and louder. Hundreds of snow geese approached our cover. As I slid under the weed covered netting and held my breath, I thought, this is either ACT II, or SCENE IV.

"I watched Lady. She was tense, alert, head up watching the birds. Dave shot, and I heard, 'Go Lady.' The wind was up, the water was choppy and I wondered how Lady could find that goose among all the decoys that looked so real. For what seemed an eternity to me, I couldn't see her, or anything that even looked like her. In my feeling of near panic, Dave assured me she was all right, and coming toward the boat, head well hidden behind the large goose held in her mouth, the rest of her body under water. I was relieved to see her come along side the boat. What a team the hunter and dog make. I can see why Dave loves that Lady!

"This was the real finale, but there remained the gathering of decoys and beating the outgoing tide back to the dock. With the outboard motor in gear, and the row boat in tow with it's full entourage, that was 'duck soup'. Guess I'll think about this part as BEHIND THE SCENES."

Juvenile brant over a grassy point . . .

Twenty years ago I did not feel that the snow geese around here exhibited much of a challenge wariness-wise. Friends who hunt them avidly still tell me to look again as today they are a good deal spookier. Due to more hunting pressure, I'd guess. While on the subject, I should be very honest and confess that a good deal of the time brant are not all wary either. Heaven forbid, but perhaps should brant be subjected to a several week season and pursued by hundreds of gunners, they'd wise-up too. Who knows? I enjoyed my combination duck/goose hunts on the South Fork but didn't go very often as the hunting pressure was considerably more than on the North Fork.

Regarding sea ducks, one time Dick Fitzner contacted Joe Welch and asked that he (Joe) recruit some friends to form a "collecting team" to shoot some ducks. Dick was a scientist with Battell Laboratories. One of the firm's field stations was in Sequim and right on the bay that bears the small town's name. Jutting out into the bay, nearly all the way across is a long, long point of land that originates from the eastern shore of the bay. This point comes within three or four hundred yards of the Sequim side of the bay. This several hundred yard interval forms a bottle-neck into Sequim Bay through which almost all sea ducks of the area pass. Sea ducks by and large do not choose to fly over solid ground if an alternate route is at hand. Dick was delegated to do a research on heavy metals in fauna of that region and one source of investigation was with sea ducks since this group of wildfowl feed principally on mollusks that live on the bottom of bays—a habitat suspected of containing heavy metals in concentration.

Dick felt that gunners stationed around the end of Sequim Point would be in a prime position to collect sea ducks. None of this "harvest" was subject to any special permits or such from Federal and or State agencies as we were bound by bag limit constraints that all hunters were held to at that point in time.

Joe enlisted Newell and me, also Tom Zmolek, a resident of the Willapa region where Joe was manager of the Willapa Wildlife Refuge. With Dick, this made a squad of five. Newell and I quickly took leadership insisting that greater success was a certainty if we employed the aid of decoys. Dick agreed so the squad sallied forth to take up temporary headquarters in a motel in Sequim. Both Newell and I took our sneakboxes and Dick furnished a skiff owned by Battell Lab. A public launch nearby furnished access and on the first morning we set forth for Sequim Point, quite close by.

Once on the point, Tom Newell and I set sea duck decoys (all hand carved by the two of us) in about equal numbers on either side of the point, yet in view of passing ducks coming into or out of the bay. We build blinds of driftwood in range of each decoy spread, divided the group, and set to work. Sea duck, divers, and now and then a puddler traded back and forth through the entrance into the bay, almost with no let up. No, the sky was not darkened by their passage, but seldom was there not a bird in view. Almost all simply passed us out of gun range, but now and then a bird would drag the decoys, and now and then one was brought to bag. We had no dog, so did all retrieving with the sneakboxes. I do not recall that we lost a single cripple.

At one point during the two days of gunning, Tom Zmolek decided for some strange reason that he "needed" to check his Browning's magazine plug. I had loaned him the gun, and cautioned him sternly that if he let the magazine spring get away from his grasp it most likely would be lost for good. You guessed it—he did, and the spring did! Much subdued Tom spent a good long while crawling about the grassy, rocky and driftwood littered area in search of it. Finally, by jingo, he did find it. I would have given big odds that he wouldn't.

Another event which livened the hunt was Joe Welch asking Tom if he could borrow his sneakbox to go out into the center channel, anchor, and hopefully intercept some of the birds that passed way out of range. Tom agreed, so Joe took off rowing out to the center of the passage. He was back in short order looking very sheepish. Seems he had arrived at spot he wanted to anchor, reached up under the fore deck, located the new twelve pound navy anchor and threw it overboard. Only problem being that it was not tied to the anchor line! Newell is to be commended that he held his temper. Perhaps not his tongue, but at least his temper. Joe never offered to reimburse Tom for the anchor and that sticks in Tom's craw still. One Christmas I sent Tom a little anchor—a decorative one made for charm bracelets. Can't recall now if Tom ever thanked me for it, but whoever said life was fair?

At hunt's end we had twenty-seven ducks in total. Species included all three scoters, both goldeneyes, several old squaw, a harlequin or two, a bufflehead or two, and one pintail. The scoters were in the majority, which were what Dick was interested in. One other happening that spiced up the hunt involved Tom Zmolek again. A bird, a rather large dark bird came right over the decoys and Tom downed it. He very proudly went out to fetch it. He brought it in, all smiles and showed it off. I held my tongue as he showed it to Joe, as I had already noted it was a black oyster catcher—a protected shore bird. Joe looked at it and blanched, his eyes wide and wild. He looked frantically about to be certain we were alone—the five of us.

Here was Joe, Superintendent of a Federal Wildlife Refuge clutching a just shot shorebird! What to do? After all options were discussed, the unanimous vote was to hide it deep in some drift pile and be done with it. This was done.

Our habitat here in Puget Sound is most attractive habitat for a great variety of shorebirds. In his fine new book, *Shorebirds of the Pacific Northwest*, Dennis Paulson stresses that our area is a shorebird haven. He states that literally millions of shorebirds in a large variety of species use the Puget Sound habitat throughout the year, with winter holding the largest populations. To hunt on the foreshore of Skagit Bay and the marshes that border South Samish Bay is to witness shorebirds in profusion. The dedicated birder must include Bowerman Basin in Grays Harbor as the shorebird area par excellence. Here during migrations, hundred of thousands of many species of shore birds stop to feed on the mud flats of this basin.

Hunting one day on the southern end of Samish Bay, I witnessed a peregrine attack on a large flock of dowitchers. As the shorebirds wheeled by my blind, the falcon appearing as though from nowhere, slashed through the outer edge of the flock. As it passed through one dowitcher dropped from the van and landed in a clump of short grass only a few feet from my blind. The falcon, after passing through the flock, bored up and onward seeming never looked back. I cannot believe the peregrine did not know it had brought a bird down, but for whatever reason did not come back. The badly injured bird hunkered in the grass clump and finally died. As the tide made, it floated off and the ever present gulls disposed of it.

Yet another time as I was in a blind hunting ducks on the Palix river marsh, I saw a falcon kill a green-winged teal from a flock of four or five. Just before the peregrine struck its chosen victim, the group of teal scattered and dove into the channel of water in front of me. The teal that the falcon struck had no chance. It appeared to be quite dead as it fell into the marsh grass. The peregrine climbed up

and away in a great arc which brought it back to where the teal lay. It spent a good while feeding on the duck. Finally satisfied, it flew off. Later, after my hunt was over, I rowed across the channel to inspect the teal. The falcon had torn some of the breast meat away and had also ripped the back feathers away and torn into the bird and eaten heart, liver, and possibly other organs. To witness first hand the attack of a falcon is cause to take one's breath away. I've seen several other falcon episodes in my years out-of-doors. Always I have marveled at the precision of these birds of prey. Bordering on the surgical.

On May 17, 1995, I sat on a drift log on Middle Sand Island in Padilla Bay. I had my motor drive Nikon and a sketch pad. My plan was to get photos of whatever struck my fancy. In May, our bays are alive with bird life. On this day a large flock of short-billed dowitchers were feeding along the shore of the sand island in company with a lone black-bellied plover in almost full breeding plumage. The dowitchers eventually moved off, but the plover stayed and fed for twenty or so minutes directly below my log, totally unaware that I hid there. As I watched and sketched the plover in haste for fear it would leave, I was struck by the almost comical attitudes it fell into as it fed. At times, almost to stand on its head. At times it felt a look about was prudent, but only the head would be raised while its body remained in the feeding posture. The plover stayed in close proximity to my log—time enough for me to make a fair number of quick sketches.

Now and again, I take the sneakbox and a passel of bluebill decoys and head to the sand islands. Between Middle Sand and Upper Sand is a deep channel that allows small boat passage on all but severe minus tides. Our big winter low tides are always at night, so this channel during duck season is always deep enough for a sneakbox. I find the potpourri of duck species that flight through this channel from the main bay and then back again to be the main ingredient for a great hunt. While both puddle ducks as well as divers pass over the channel, it is mostly the divers that provide the bulk of the shooting. Puddlers fly through too high to make it all worthwhile. The divers are mainly bluebills, but goldeneyes and buffleheads are also common. Greater scaup make up the bulk of our bluebills on Padilla and this species is indeed a fine duck. Almost as large as the redhead and fine of flesh, I find the "big bluebills" of Padilla worth pursuing. Here in this channel, I put out thirty or so bluebill blocks and net the boat over and anchor it along the shore parallel to the channel. Sometimes the divers land but more frequently it is a pass shooting show. The decoys simply draw them over into range of the gun. There is feed up in the little bay behind the islands and this is why they have a through ticket. Sometimes I've made a one species hunt in this channel. It is a lot of fun. I use such rules as, drakes only, bluebills only, or the same with buffleheads.

On the north end of the Middle island still stands a wooden blind. Very dilapidated now, but when I first saw it in 1979 it was a handsome structure. A sketch here portrays the blind when I saw it first. I have no idea who was the blind's builder. I've inquired through the years with no success. In any event, I've gunned from the blind with decoys set in the little bay in front. This is a high tide affair and for me has not proven to be as productive as layout in the channel on a lower tide.

One special hunt in this channel between the islands stands out above all the others I've made there. This day was one with heavy rain, but little or no winds. The heavy downpour reduced visibility so much that the puddle ducks also flew quite low. As usual I had a rig of bluebill decoys out and they drew the puddle ducks over in range as well as the divers. There were so many puddle ducks on the move through the channel that I decided to shoot mallard drakes only. As I recall the limit that season was six. All went well until the rain slacked off about the time I had bagged my fourth greenhead. As if on cue, the puddlers all gained altitude through the slot and that was all she wrote so far as a limit of greenheads. Oh well, still better than a poke in the eye with a sharp stick. Happy with it all, I picked up and went home.

Another hunt of Middle Sand, this time from the old blind, sticks in my memory. It was early in the season, almost like Indian Summer so common here in early October. I don't remember anything much at all about the shooting, the bag, or other trivia. What I do remember well is that I witnessed one whale of a lot of migrating white-fronted geese. They were coming out of the north, straight down bay, one flock after another—some right over my head. But high. No chance for any shooting. Flock after flock they came and for a while—maybe about fifteen minutes or more several thousand specs flew over my blind in this short time—and then they were gone. No straggler flocks. When the last bunch passed that was all. I shall

a grey belly close aboard. Decoys are Custom Bilt circa 1970. View is from the layout boat . . .

never forget that passage of geese. Reminiscent of the hordes one can expect to see in Klamath Country, or Louisiana or Nebraska, or…

These sand islands hold my interest as they are close by and well suited for sneakbox work. As long as I'm able, I'll be going to the Sands now and then.

In the little town of Bayview, only two miles from our home up here on Bayview Ridge, is a very fine concrete boat ramp and a fine parking lot. Paved. Really "uptown". Only problem, is that it takes a plus seven feet of water to float a boat at the ramp's bottom. For almost a mile out from the launch is one vast mud flat. When the tide book says 7.0 feet of water, I launch my sneakbox and can know I have about two hours of water before the 9.0 high and then another hour and a half before I need to be back at the ramp hauling my out my sneakbox. Why go to all the bother, you ask? Simply beause hundreds of bluebills and thousands of wigeons use the east side of Padilla Bay for rest and feed. A portion of this eastern shoreline is a refuge. Here, at times, there are tens of thousands of resting ducks. The water is black with 'em. For my operation here off Bayview, I row—don't even take an outboard. Once in the water, the decks piled with decoys—bluebills and wigeon, I simply row straight out towards the far bay shore, about a quarter of a mile. Here in five or so feet of water, I rig the bluebills in one group, the wigeon in another. Alongside, the sneakbox is anchored, netted, and several gulls added to the decks. Without an outboard engine on the transom, the sneakbox takes on an entirely new and lower profile. This is the way the sneakbox is meant to be used when Cap Seamen designed the first one on Fishing Creek, New Jersey in 1837. With no engine, the sneakbox grassed or netted over comes about as close to a sinkbox as one can get—legally. If the birds are trading from the refuge to the south end of the bay, the action, laid out off Bayview, can be as the young say, 'awesome!'

Weather is a big factor here. Five feet of water churns up pretty good if the wind comes up. Especially if it's blowing against the flow of the tide. It also churns up FAST! On a couple of occasions I was hard pressed to pick up and row back only a quarter mile when one of these flurries came up. Other times the birds simply don't move. Oh sure, the buffies always do, but I find little interest in shooting buffleheads unless I have rigged my bufflehead decoys for that purpose. Now this is a hunt, rather than an opportunistic shoot—drakes only. I most likely enjoy the Bayview layout so much because I can row out there. Anymore, I can't walk very well, but by jimminies, I can still row.

And I fully plan to be rowing off Bayview during the waterfowl season in the year 2000. It will be my 71st season. I am already planning my decoy rig—something special.

The Edison Hunting Club was formed in 1931. It
consisted of 180 acres – some marginal pasture,
some tide flats, and some frontage on the Samish
river delta, and the remainder on the South end of
Samish Bay. The club's "house" and bunk house are
drawn here as I first saw them in 1985.

The "family" blind is depicted here. It is extant and is
located on the western side of the club. It fronts on
that area where the Samish river and bay waters merge.
Anson Brooks explained to me, that this blind was so
named as all family members, no matter what age,
could easily reach this blind — even in street shoes!

This is the West blind. It is shown here on a low tide.
Here too, the name makes reference to it's location on
that boundary of the club on the shore of Samish
bay. This blind was used for brant hunting and was
also a fine location for wigeon. It was destroyed
by storms in 1991 and never replaced. It is shown
here as I sketched it in 1986.

This brant blind is located on the northern side of the
Club that fronts on the broad expanse of Samish bay.
This is the original as I sketched it in 1986. This
blind was carried away by wind and wave in 1989, but
later replaced by Tony Breckenridge, "as much like the
original as I could make it", Tony told me. The old
blind is shown here on a moderately high tide.

I first sketched and photographed this aging shed circa 1985. At a later time Tony unlocked the door to show me a pile of old hand carved brant decoys. Of equal interest to me was an old paper tacked to a wall near the door. Scrawled on this paper were dates put down by the caretaker indicating when he had last fed the Club's live decoys! It was aptly named the Granary.

CHAPTER 10

The Now

ONLY LAST MONTH I blew out seventy-seven candles on my birthday cake. My plans for the future you ask? How about more of the same? Only, please, at a much reduced pace! I enjoy painting as much as ever, and decoy carving when I am able, holds the same fascination. Outdoor activities on the water and in the field lure me still.

After Dwight Schuh and I collaborated on *The Bottoms* in 1987, I found working on book production opened a new interest for me. On and off through the years, I did illustrations for Worth Mathewson's articles on hunting. It followed in a natural way that we got around to collaborating on books. First on his *Big December Canvasbacks* in 1997 and this year on *Waterfowling These Past 50 Years, Especially Brant*. I personally am having the time of my life with books, and look forward to working with Sand Lake Press in publishing others.

I seem to have the tendency to plan projects to death—a trait that carries over even into my waterfowling. This coming season I'll be trying a new (for me) style of decoy hunting for puddle ducks. With our duck season barely closed, I have already several detailed drawings of moving decoy rigs, portable light-weight blinds, and a few feather-light balsa decoys. I am also looking forward to shooting my Winchester 42 once again at ducks. My friend, Ron Saylor, will load three inch shells for me using bismuth number six shot. For puddlers over decoys at twenty-five yards this will be like old times on the Willamette River in the '60s. This is the sort of good stuff that never lets time hang heavy for me.

Frequently, since Lady died, I have hot flashes to get another gunning dog. One time I feel like a bird dog would be a great choice. We could go over the mountains together and have great times up in N.E. Washington hunting the several species of upland birds there. Almost as quickly, I come back to earth, and face the fact, that for me, the walking required to hunt upland is out of the question anymore. It would not be fair to an eager bird dog to be saddled with me so that settles that. Then another time my thoughts focus on another duck dog, but again I simply could not take a retriever amarsh enough times each season to be fair to the dog. Solution to this? Listen to Delphie's wishes and get a terrier. In our case, we now have Cisy, a little five pound Yorkie. A hyper little imp that has captivated us totally. As I throw a ball for her to retrieve the notion frequently crosses my mind—would she be able to fetch in a snipe or dove? A teal perhaps? Hmmmm—and so it goes.

I've painted sporting scenes for so many years that not to be able to sit in my studio working on a watercolor is impossible to imagine. So, I plan to just keep plugging away doing all of the fun things that I can. It's a great world, eh? You know, I think I'll load a bunch of decoys in the sneakbox and go down to the Bayview launch tomorrow morning. I'll row out and set up a rig and "meet 'em coming head on!"

The End